U. S. Joint Forces Command
JOINT WARFIGHTING CENTER
116 LAKE VIEW PARKWAY
SUFFOLK, VA 23435-2697

MESSAGE TO JOINT WARFIGHTERS

Persistent surveillance, as currently defined in joint doctrine, is a collection strategy that emphasizes the ability of some collection systems to linger on demand in an area to detect, locate, characterize, identify, track, target, and possibly provide battle damage assessment and retargeting in near or real-time. Persistent surveillance facilitates the prediction of an adversary's behavior and the formulation and execution of preemptive activities to deter or forestall anticipated adversary courses of action.

An effectively executed persistent surveillance strategy greatly enhances joint military operations. However, warfighter challenges (WFC) nominated by combatant commands and the military services and lessons learned from the field indicate that persistent surveillance needs to be improved. Persistent surveillance missions and processes being used by the joint force today do not effectively keep pace with operational need and are not adequately documented. The current joint persistent surveillance process is ad-hoc, cumbersome, and unresponsive. Data is available in abundance, but the joint warfighter is starving for actionable information required to support operations to the tactical edge. The current process does not support the timely and accurate assessment of collected data, limiting the joint force's ability to dynamically re-task assets. The joint force commander (JFC) requires adequate capability to rapidly integrate and focus national to tactical collection assets to achieve the persistent surveillance of a designated geographic area or a specific mission set.

With these WFCs and four primary expected outcomes in mind, Joint Doctrine Support Division and Solution Evaluation Division, supported by the Services, have experimented on various facets of joint integrated persistent surveillance (JIPS) over the last two years. This handbook describes the results of this effort, and includes considerations for planning, executing, and assessing JIPS. In particular, it highlights how the JFC can better command and support persistent surveillance operations to the tactical level through effective capability apportionment and management; timely and responsive analytic support; and fast, reliable command and control. This handbook is intended to give designated JFCs, their component commanders, and their respective staffs an informative source of information related to persistent surveillance operations.

We hope this handbook stimulates the joint community's thinking about how to address JIPS' challenges. We encourage you to use the information in this handbook and provide feedback to help us capture value-added ideas for incorporation in emerging joint doctrine, training, and professional military education.

JOSEPH REYNES, JR.
Major General, USAF
Assistant Deputy Director
Joint Development

1. Scope

This handbook provides pre-doctrinal guidance on the planning, execution, and assessment of joint integrated persistent surveillance (JIPS) by a joint task force (JTF) and its components. Significant prior work has been done in support of persistent intelligence, surveillance, and reconnaissance (ISR) and much of the information in this handbook was gleaned from that data. However, the scope of this handbook pertains to the subset of persistent surveillance: the processes which contribute to creating a persistent surveillance strategy and those required for executing persistent surveillance missions. The document serves as a bridge between current best practices in the field and incorporation of value-added ideas in joint doctrine.

2. Purpose

This handbook draws on current doctrine, useful results from relevant studies and experimentation, and recognized best practices. It presents some challenges of persistent surveillance to include capability gaps and some potential solutions to these shortfalls, especially in the areas of planning and preparation, managing requirements and tasking, visualization and tracking, and assessment of persistent surveillance missions. It also offers some considerations for the future development of JIPS-related joint doctrine, training, materiel (logistics), leadership education, personnel, facility planning, and policy (DOTMLPF-P).

3. Application

This handbook is based on joint lessons and Service learned data; joint, multinational, and Service doctrine and procedures; training and education material from CAPSTONE, KEYSTONE, and PINNACLE senior executive education programs; joint and Service exercise observations, facilitated after-action reviews and commander's summary reports; related joint concepts; experimentation results; joint exercises and trip reports; joint publication assessment reports; research from advanced concept/joint capability technology development projects and capability development documentation for acquisition programs, and DOTMLPF-P change recommendations. This handbook also includes the results of a two-year analysis and experimentation effort conducted by Joint Doctrine Support Division and Solution Evaluation Division, with participation by all the Services. The JIPS project was driven by the following military problem statement: "The JFC requires adequate capability to rapidly integrate and focus national to tactical collection assets to achieve the persistent surveillance of a designated geographic area or a specific mission set." The genesis/mandate was that five of the top 40 FY 09-10 priority warfighter challenges (WFCs) require persistent surveillance solutions (WFCs 2, 4, 13, 20, 30) as reported by USPACOM, USCENTCOM, and the Marine Corps Combat Development Command. Experimentation included a stakeholder conference; baseline assessment; a constructive simulation effort; a "human-in-the-loop" experiment; and a multi-Service, coalition, live-fly environment experiment that simulated operations in

Afghanistan (EMPIRE CHALLENGE 2010). Development of the JIPS handbook is tied to the four major outcomes from experimentation and reflects concepts of operations developed for the proposed DOTMLPF-P change recommendation submission.

4. Command

This handbook is a pre-doctrinal, non-authoritative supplement to joint doctrine that can help JTF and component commanders and their staffs plan for and support persistent surveillance operations. The information herein also helps the joint community develop doctrine and mature emerging concepts for possible transition into joint doctrine. Commanders should consider the benefits and risks of using this information in actual operations.

5. Contact Information

Comments and suggestions on this important topic are welcomed. The Solution Evaluation Division point of contact is Lieutenant Colonel Stan Murphy, USA, john.murphy@jfcom.mil (757) 203-3477 (DSN 668) or Mr. Tom Donahue, GS-14, tom.donahue@jfcom.mil, (757) 203-3347 (DSN 668). The Joint Doctrine Support Division points of contact are Lieutenant Colonel Jeffrey Martin, USAF, jeffrey.martin@jfcom.mil, (757) 203-6871 (DSN 668) and Ms. Rebecca Sorell, (757) 203-5513, rebecca.sorell@jfcom.mil (DSN 668).

TABLE OF CONTENTS

FIGURES

TABLES

Intentionally Blank

CHAPTER I
PERSISTENT SURVEILLANCE CHALLENGES

"The enemy is so well hidden that it takes multiple sources of intelligence to corroborate one another.

- *Signals Intelligence (SIGINT), for example, can locate a target but may not be able to discern who it is.*
- *Full Motion Video (FMV) can track but not necessarily identify.*
- *Human Intelligence (HUMINT) can provide intent but may not be able to fix a target to a precise location.*
- *Airborne Intelligence, Surveillance, and Reconnaissance (ISR)'s effectiveness grows exponentially when it is cued to and driven by other sources of intelligence rather than operating alone.*

Without a robust, collaborative intelligence network to guide it, sensors are often used in reactive modes that negate their true power and tend to minimize their full potential.

These intelligence disciplines provide a start point into the enemy network that can be exploited through persistent and patient observation."

Flynn, M.T., Juergens, R., Cantrell, T.L.
Employing ISR: Special Operations Forces (SOF) Best Practices
Joint Force Quarterly, Third Quarter 2008

1. Problem Statement

a. Persistent surveillance missions and processes used by the joint force today do not effectively keep pace with operational needs. The current processes are ad-hoc, not codified adequately in joint doctrine, and are therefore not responsive in today's operational environment. These ad-hoc processes coupled with improvements in technology leave the joint warfighter "starving" for actionable information while drowning in data.

b. The joint force commander (JFC) requires the means to rapidly integrate and synchronize national through tactical level collection assets to achieve persistent surveillance of a specific area or target of interest.

c. A persistent surveillance mission is directed by a commander on a specific, high priority target that is determined to be mission essential and supports the scheme of maneuver, commander's guidance, and intent.

d. Recommendations for improving persistent surveillance missions (Figure I-1) are:

(1) Improve joint persistent surveillance asset integration through streamlining the tipping, cueing, and communications procedures among collection assets.

(2) Efficient use of collection assets to achieve persistent surveillance in restricted and denied areas.

(3) Improve doctrine, organization, and tactics, techniques and procedures (TTPs) for the JFC to enable command and control of joint intelligence, surveillance and reconnaissance (ISR) operations down to the tactical level.

(4) Develop a process for assessment of persistent surveillance missions.

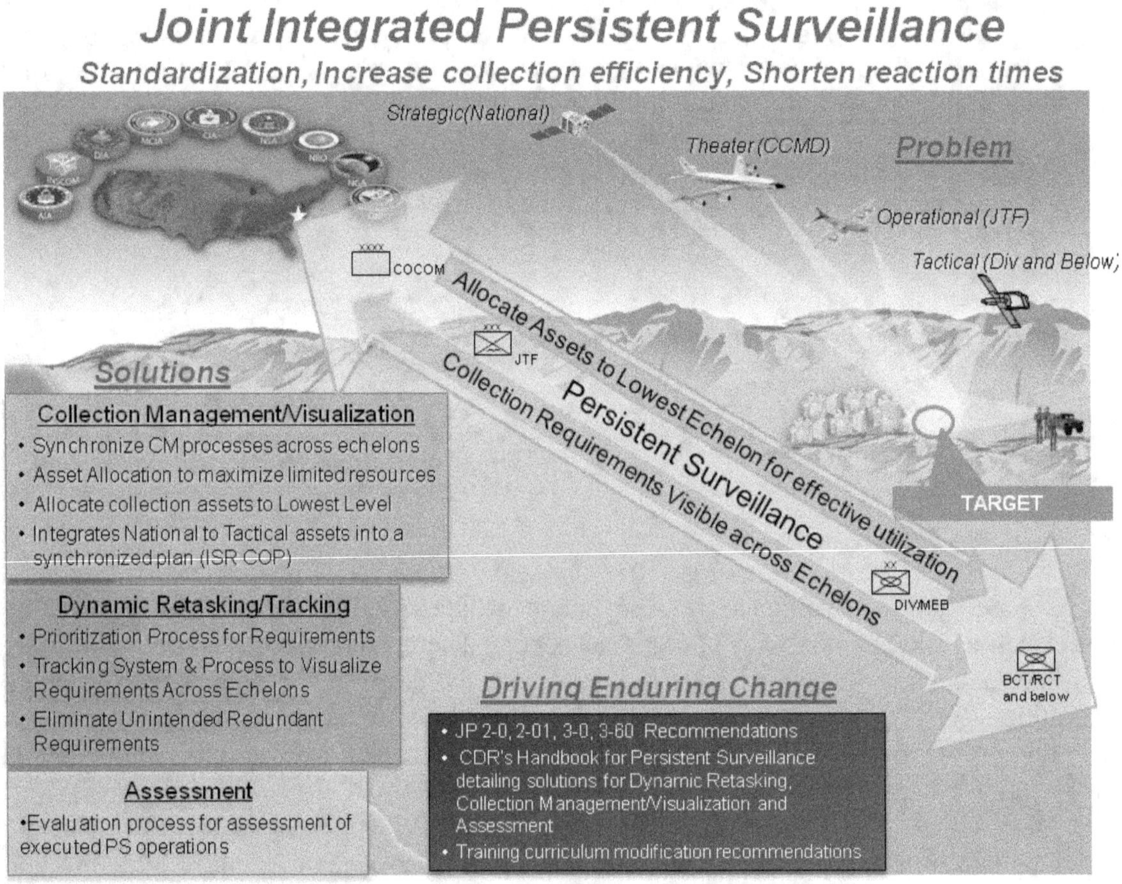

Figure I-1. Joint Integrated Persistent Surveillance

2. Capability Shortfalls

a. A review of the existing ISR related documents served as a basis for identifying current practices, processes, knowledge, and understanding related to persistent surveillance operations. The starting point for examining shortfalls for persistent surveillance was a review of the joint term "Persistent Surveillance" from Joint Publication (JP) 1-02, *Department of Defense Dictionary of Military and Associated Terms*, which provided the following definition:

"*A collection strategy that emphasizes the ability of some collection systems to linger on demand in an area to detect, locate, characterize, identify, track, target, and possibly provide battle damage assessment and retargeting in near or real-time. Persistent surveillance facilitates the prediction of an adversary's behavior and the formulation and execution of preemptive activities to deter or forestall anticipated adversary courses of action."*

b.   After review of documents related to persistent surveillance and collaboration with combatant commands, Services, and other stakeholders, it was apparent the current definition of "Persistent Surveillance" falls short of commander's requirements across all echelons. A revised definition of persistent surveillance has been submitted for inclusion in updates to joint publications as follows:

"An ISR strategy to achieve surveillance of a priority target that is constant or of sufficient duration and frequency to provide the joint force commander the information to act in a timely manner."

c.   The rationale for the recommended change is to state clearly and succinctly, the definition of persistent surveillance, who it is for and what it accomplishes. The term *'area'* in the current doctrinal definition is not as descriptive or inclusive as *'target'* in the recommended change to the definition. In the recommended definition, the term "target" is doctrinally explained as, *"In intelligence usage, a country, area, installation, agency, or person against which intelligence operations are directed."* This change expands and more clearly defines what persistent surveillance is to accomplish. The inclusion of, *"to provide the joint force commander with the information required to act in a timely manner,"* is directly aligned with commanders involvement at all command levels by providing guidance, intent, and end state objectives that help to shape the ISR strategy; *allowing the full incorporation of all assets and methods available and suitable.* The ultimate goal of persistent surveillance is to provide the commander vital information at a critical moment in order to make timely decisions that allow joint forces to achieve their objectives. **Planning for persistent surveillance is part of several joint processes:**

(1) **joint intelligence preparation of the operational environment (JIPOE)** to include predicting an adversary's behavior;

(2) participation in the **joint operation planning process (JOPP)** for planning and executing friendly actions to achieve desired effects (this includes development of the ISR synchronization plan); and

(3) input to the **joint targeting cycle** for selection and prioritization of targets.

For more information on the three joint processes, see Chapter III, "Preparation and Planning."

d.   In addition to a shortfall regarding the existing persistent surveillance definition, several capability gaps and shortfalls were identified through a detailed review of over

130 pertinent documents. The following is a list of necessary corrections to the identified capability gaps and shortfalls:

    (1) Improve collection planning across all echelons

    (2) Improve collection assets visibility

    (3) Improve collection requirements visibility

    (4) Reduce unintentional redundancy of collection assets

    (5) Implement a cross-echelon prioritization scheme

    (6) Improve intelligence, information and data visibility

    (7) Improve the dynamic ad hoc re-tasking process.

    e.   Addressing these shortfalls will help improve the joint intelligence, joint operation planning and execution, and joint targeting processes; as well as assist in achieving the collection objective for persistent surveillance.

3. Addressing Shortfalls

    a.   In examining joint integrated persistent surveillance (JIPS) mission planning, three enabling themes regarding visibility emerged as follows: 1) ISR asset visibility; 2) collection requirements visibility at multiple echelons; and 3) intelligence, information, and data visibility. Each organization that assisted in examining JIPS planning had its own perspective; however, the issues they identified could all be linked to the above themes. Many organizations cited shortcomings and capability gaps in persistent surveillance planning, but very few had a grasp of the scope of persistent surveillance enabling capabilities and the various issues that required resolution in order to successfully conduct persistent surveillance missions.

    (1) **ISR Asset Visibility**. Collection managers require awareness, across all echelons, of the ISR assets that may be brought to bear on collection planning. Commanders and staffs also require this capacity to better plan and synchronize operations. From the operational to tactical levels, planners must know what ISR assets are currently conducting missions, what their specific collection tasks are, who manages these assets through either operational control (OPCON) or tactical control (TACON), and the future availability of these assets. Visibility of ISR assets enhances planning by enabling integration and synchronization of collection tasks which reduces redundancy of similar collection requirements. It also enhances cross-cueing of ISR assets by allowing commanders to seize opportunities by understanding options for cross-cueing with regard to asset availability.

(2) **Collection Requirements Visibility**. Collection managers require visibility and awareness of collection requirements not only within their area of operations (AO), but within adjacent areas, and also the requirements of their higher headquarters. Visibility of collection requirements across all echelons is necessary to allow planners to combine redundant requirements and make best use of the available collection capacity. Visibility of existing collection requirements across all echelons is a significant required capability in planning persistent surveillance missions. Collection managers should be able to view all collection requirements and pending collection tasks related to current and planned operations. This will assist them in recognizing duplication of collection efforts and eliminate unintentional redundancy within an ISR strategy by enabling the combining of similar collection requests into a single requirement. Collection requirement traceability from the originator, through the planning, collection, exploitation and dissemination processes, and tracking the collected information back to the user will allow assessment of effectiveness and timeliness of the collection effort.

(3) **Intelligence, Information, and Data Visibility**. Having broad visibility of all intelligence, information, and data products provides significant benefits to persistent surveillance planning. This visibility will assist intelligence directors and collection managers to more effectively plan, prepare, execute, and assess persistent surveillance missions. Intelligence, information, and data visibility will also improve operations planning, target development, and data correlation to enhance cross-cueing opportunities during current operations. Visibility of intelligence, information, and data can also reduce unnecessary collection tasks by satisfying collection requirements with information that has already been collected.

b. Past studies on persistent surveillance identified stove-piped organizations and processes which inhibited leveraging all surveillance asset providers. Successful persistent surveillance was achieved when the collection and production activities of the ISR mission package were synchronized and the results of these activities were fully integrated with the commander's decision points in the military operation.

c. Lessons learned from the operational to tactical levels highlight the need to expedite dynamic re-tasking of collection capabilities, in order to support persistent surveillance operations. This is a complex issue due to the technical, organizational, and tactics, techniques, and procedures (TTP) requirements at the multiple echelons who have OPCON and tasking authority of the collections assets that may be required for dynamic or ad hoc re-tasking, coupled with the need for quick action.

d. A clear demand exists for persistent surveillance capabilities at each warfighting echelon. Many significant persistent surveillance capability gaps exist, but there is no coordinated plan for closing these gaps. In today's operational environment (OE) various organizations developing or investigating persistent surveillance solutions loosely interact as required, often in an ineffective manner, to satisfy their immediate needs for resources or information. Lack of centralized coordination and recognized methodology in planning persistent surveillance missions often results in overlapping or redundant collection efforts that do not satisfy the commander's requirements.

e. Improving collaboration between the operational and tactical levels through integrated and synchronized collection planning and operations, supported by the three visualization themes articulated above, will facilitate implementation of strategies that leverage collection assets in support of persistent surveillance requirements of the joint task force (JTF) or its major subordinate elements.

4. Examining Definitions

See Figure I-2 for an overview of the discussions below.

a. **Surveillance versus Persistent Surveillance**

(1) Along with examining problems with the existing definition for Persistent Surveillance, it is also useful to conduct a comparison between the proposed definition for persistent surveillance and the definition for surveillance.

(a) Surveillance is defined as the systematic observation of aerospace, surface, or subsurface areas, places, persons, or things, by visual, aural, electronic, photographic, or other means.

(b) Persistent surveillance is defined in our proposed definition as an ISR strategy to achieve surveillance of a priority target that is constant or of sufficient duration and frequency to provide the joint force commander with the information required to act in a timely manner.

(2) Aside from time (duration and frequency), the fundamental difference between the two definitions is that persistent surveillance is an ISR strategy. Surveillance, as defined, isn't a strategy, but it is conducted over a period of time and with available capabilities. A strategy is defined in Merriam-Webster's Dictionary as, "a careful plan or method; and the art of devising or employing plans according to a goal." Persistent surveillance is just that – an art, a design, a careful method, and it is focused on a goal – to provide the joint force commander with the information required to make a decision. The art of creating an effective ISR strategy can be accomplished when a commander and staff fully understand the available collection capabilities; understand the OE to include the adversary and the effect on the collection capability; and, understand the intelligence requirements, thus designing an effective and efficient strategy to employ combinations of available collection capabilities in the right places and times to gain the required information.

b. **Persistent Surveillance vs. Persistent ISR**

(1) The terms "persistent surveillance" and "persistent ISR" are at times used interchangeably. The *Persistent Intelligence, Surveillance, and Reconnaissance:*

Planning and Direction Joint Integrating Concept, introduced the term persistent ISR in an effort to improve persistence through integrated, synchronized management of planning and direction of the ISR Enterprise, including all intelligence disciplines, such as human intelligence, imagery intelligence (IMINT), SIGINT, measurement and signature intelligence (MASINT), open-source intelligence (OSINT), as well as non-traditional ISR collection capabilities. This term does not differ greatly from the JIPS proposed definition of "persistent surveillance."

Figure I-2. Persistent Surveillance Lexicon Differences and Commonalities

Intentionally Blank

CHAPTER II
THE HUMAN ELEMENT IN PERSISTENT SURVEILLANCE

"Persistent surveillance has a better chance of success if it adopts the principle of the human-centric system. The individual warfighter... is the one on whom our operational goals rise or fall and is the key element in any military machine. And, with sensors now occupying a vital place in the force, that human must be at the focal point before, during and after sensors are designed and deployed."

Herbert A. Brown
VADM USN (Ret.)
Sensors and Sensibility
Signal Online, April 2006

1. Persistent Surveillance Overview

a. Persistent surveillance missions do not occur in a vacuum; rather, they are tied to a commander's mission, intent, commander's critical information requirements (CCIRs), and the overall collection plan. Any persistent surveillance mission has to be managed within the confines of commander's guidance and intent for that operation within the context of the overall unit mission.

b. Persistent surveillance missions can last for days and may require constant surveillance from multiple assets working in a synchronized manner. This is especially true when considering 24 hour operations (where assets may operate in shifts) and down time is a planning factor. Planners and collection managers have to maintain an objective view of the trade-off of costs to other collection requirements and the benefits of assigning assets to a specific mission. A recommendation may have to be made to the commander to end a persistent surveillance mission that is too expensive in terms of asset hours or loss of collection against other priority requirements.

c. Persistent surveillance missions require the active involvement of commanders and their operations and intelligence staffs. Commanders of all echelons involved in persistent surveillance mission planning must determine the priority of their mission as it relates to the operations of their higher headquarters. Persistent surveillance missions potentially take a large amount of time and result in tasking of multiple assets and must be assessed against other operational and intelligence missions in the area of operations. The commander's priority of effort must be conveyed to the staff officers who have tasking authority over the required operational and intelligence assets.

d. Each persistent surveillance mission evolution requires detailed planning and focus on a chain of collection tasks that need to be synchronized and managed as a coherent whole. This "system-of-systems" approach to persistent surveillance missions is in itself a part of a larger collections system. The proper management and prioritization of requirements, combined with detailed situational understanding of the ongoing operation, and rapid identification and resolution of deficiencies or gaps in collection during the mission, are necessary to meet the needs of the commander in a successful persistent surveillance mission.

e.   Changes in the target or asset availability must be instantly communicated to all interested parties, including commanders, asset managers and the responsible operations center. The establishment and maintenance of a common operational picture (COP), or user defined operational picture (UDOP) available to all required personnel at multiple echelons, is absolutely vital to conducting successful persistent surveillance missions.

f.   There are many possible reasons for the dynamic re-tasking of an asset to support a persistent surveillance mission. It is not always possible to predict when re-tasking is required; however, a good understanding of the OE can support smoother and more efficient re-tasking opportunities. Operational staffs should prepare as much as possible in order to rapidly and effectively conduct dynamic re-taskings should the need arise. Re-tasking issues are discussed in Chapter IV, "Managing Requirements and Tasking."

g.   Commanders can greatly reduce the time required to act on an immediate re-tasking requirement by maintaining awareness of environmental changes, other ongoing operations, and other assets in the area that could be used in a dynamic re-tasking situation. A shared COP/UDOP is a vital tool to rapidly identify necessary situations for re-tasking and to effectively coordinate between higher, lower and adjacent units.

h.   While conducting persistent surveillance missions, there is always the possibility that a staff will have target fixation and concentrate on the ongoing mission while ignoring or downplaying other requirements. The persistent surveillance target has to be viewed in relation to the "big picture" of the overall operation. Throughout the life of a persistent surveillance mission, there will be many additional requirements that will have to be dealt with and incorporated into ongoing collection operations.

i.   Commanders and decision makers must be aware at all times of the other high priority requirements that are being addressed in their area of operation, influence and interest. This will help identify what units and intelligence assets are unavailable for dynamic re-tasking requirements, and also if some higher priority event could call for the cancellation of the persistent surveillance mission and the refocusing of previously tasked assets on that new requirement.

2.   Determining Mission End State

a.   An end state is the set of required conditions that defines achievement of the commander's objectives. Commanders should define their intended end state of a persistent surveillance mission. Once defined, the staff can determine what information needs to be collected before, during, and after the operation in order to assess it. This list needs to be promulgated to all involved commands. A well articulated end state will support the development of metrics by staff officers that will determine the level of success of the mission, so that a proper assessment of the operation can be conducted.

b. The specific time requirement for a persistent surveillance mission may be undefined; however, a decision can be made as to what constitutes the start and completion of the mission. If the mission is created by a tip or other unconfirmed piece of information, a commander can designate that the mission start immediately or he may wait until intelligence has confirmed the source, or use another trigger such as when the target moves or activates.

c. Every echelon needs to know what the required end state is for the particular mission. Persistent surveillance is an operational mission; therefore, the commander will most likely declare the end state as an operational action (e.g., target destroyed, individual captured), rather than as an intelligence end state where a specific piece of information is gathered (i.e., priority intelligence requirement [PIR] satisfied). For example, a mission concerning a high-value target (HVT) reported in a denied area would be officially initiated when the HVT is reported at a location. It would continue until such a time as the commander could operationally act through killing or capturing the HVT.

3. Commander's Responsibilities

a. Commanders are more than just consumers of intelligence. Commanders drive the planning, direction and conduct of intelligence operations (Figure II-1). Commanders organize their staffs and assign responsibilities as necessary to ensure unity of effort in persistent surveillance missions. Additionally, they must continuously provide feedback on the effectiveness of persistent surveillance in supporting operations.

b. **Understand Intelligence Doctrine, Capabilities, and Limitations**. Commanders must know intelligence doctrine, and understand intelligence discipline capabilities and limitations, as well as intelligence procedures and products. A firm understanding of the capabilities and their availability allows a commander a better understanding of the requirements for conducting persistent surveillance operations while continuing daily missions, including overall collection operations. Although intelligence analysis provides the necessary basis for operational planning, it must be understood that all operations entail a degree of risk. It is the commander's responsibility to assess that risk while approving persistent surveillance missions.

c. **Provide Planning Guidance**. Commanders focus the planning process through the commander's intent, planning guidance, and initial CCIRs. The commander's guidance provides the basis for the concept of intelligence operations, coherent target development and identifying missions requiring persistent surveillance.

d. **Define the Area of Interest**. Commanders should define their areas of interest based on mission analysis, their concept of operations (CONOPS), and a preliminary assessment of relevant aspects of the operational environment (prepared as part of the JIPOE process, explained in the following chapter).

Figure II-1. Commander's Responsibilities: Emphasis on Persistent Surveillance Missions

e. **Identify Critical Intelligence Needs**. Commanders should identify their CCIRs, to include PIRs with associated decision points, as early as possible in order to facilitate intelligence planning and synchronization with operations. Commanders should not only specify what information is needed, but also when and how long it is needed in order to be integrated into operational planning.

f. **Integrate Intelligence in Plans and Operations**. Commanders are ultimately responsible for ensuring that persistent surveillance is fully integrated into their plans and operations. The successful synchronization of persistence operations with all other elements of joint operations occurs in the Joint Operations Center (JOC) and begins with commanders providing their intent and desired end state for persistent surveillance missions in the earliest stages of the joint operation planning process.

g. **Proactively Engage the Intelligence Staff**. Commanders should actively engage their intelligence officers in discussions of the adversary, force protection concerns, and future operations. Frequent consultations between the JFC and the joint force's intelligence staff facilitate situational awareness, particularly a mutual understanding regarding where and when persistent surveillance is required.

h. **Demand High Quality, Predictive Intelligence**. Commanders must hold their intelligence personnel accountable for providing predictive intelligence that meets all the attributes of intelligence. However, JFCs must also understand the challenges and limitations that confront intelligence personnel in assessing adversary intentions and future course of actions (COAs).

4. **Joint Force Intelligence Staff's Responsibilities**

a. In broad terms, the J2 assists the commander in developing strategy, planning operations and campaigns, and tasking intelligence assets, for effective joint and unified operations. The J2 is specifically responsible for determining the requirements and direction needed to ensure unity of the intelligence effort and to support the commander's objectives/end state. The J2's responsibility also includes applying national intelligence capabilities, optimizing the utilization of joint force intelligence assets, and identifying and integrating additional intelligence resources. Persistent surveillance missions are a fusion of intelligence and operations and the J2 is a critical element in the planning, coordination and execution of these missions. Among the J2's major responsibilities, the following (Figure II-2) are established and the recommended tasks to support successful persistent surveillance missions: [1]

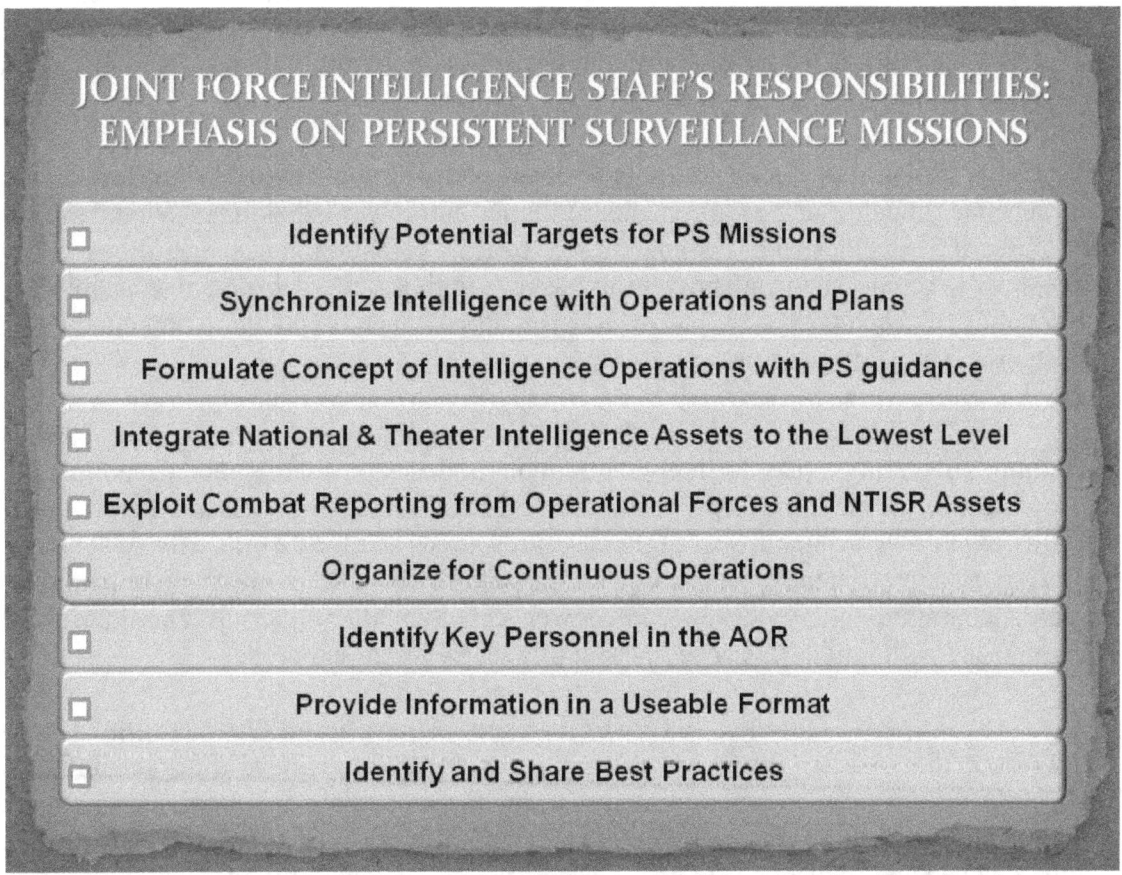

Figure II-2. Joint Force Intelligence Staff's Responsibilities: Emphasis on Persistence Surveillance Missions

b.   The recommended nine tasks to support successful surveillance missions are:

(1) **Identifying Potential Targets for Persistent Surveillance (PS) Missions**. Using the JIPOE process (discussed in further detail in Chapter 3) as a basis, the J2 is responsible for analyzing all relevant aspects of the OE, determining adversary capabilities and estimating adversary intentions. This process is crucial to successful determination of key nodes and potential targets. The J2 also provides the resulting threat assessments and warning to the joint force and its components, and maintains a continuous dialog with the JFC concerning the adversary's relative strengths, weaknesses, and ability to prevent the joint force from accomplishing its mission.

(2) **Synchronize Intelligence With Operations and Plans**. The J2 must ensure that intelligence collection, processing, exploitation, analysis, and dissemination activities are planned, sequenced, and timed to support the commander's decision-making process, and to meet the requirements of planners. This is particularly important in the field of persistent surveillance, which provides a functional link between intelligence and operations, as it may require coordinating traditional collection assets with non-traditional assets and operational capabilities. The commanders' desired effects provide the basis for identifying persistent surveillance missions, while assessment will inform any changes in the commander's objective and strategy.

(3) **Formulate Concept of Intelligence Operations with PS guidance**. To communicate guidance and requirements to higher and lower echelons of command, the joint force J2 develops and disseminates a concept of intelligence operations. The concept will include such information as tasking authorities, reporting responsibilities, coordinating between teams, etc. and must provide guidance on planning and conducting persistent surveillance missions.

(4) **Integrate National and Theater Intelligence Assets to the Lowest Echelon**. The J2 must plan to integrate national and theater intelligence capabilities to the lowest level in the joint force. Units at the brigade/regiment level and below might not fully exploit the availability of higher level resources and the J2 must ensure available assets are used in efficient ways throughout the joint force. The J2 must ensure persistent surveillance missions are feasible for lower echelons that otherwise could not be accomplished without the J2's access, capability, capacity, or expertise.

(5) **Exploit Combat Reporting from Operational Forces and Non-Traditional ISR Assets**. Forward and engaged combat forces have a responsibility to report information that can be integrated with intelligence; their unique access is proven exceptionally valuable. Likewise, special operations forces (SOF) provide the JFC with a unique manned and unmanned "eyes-on-target" deep look capability, especially useful in areas where other sensors are not available, or can't provide required "resolution." Persistent surveillance, being extremely resource intensive, should not depend solely on airborne ISR and requires coordination with non-traditional capabilities to be successful.

(6) **Organize for Continuous Operations**. Persistent surveillance missions can require 24-hour support over the course of several days and the joint force's intelligence organizations should be structured for continuous day-night and all-weather operations. The J-2's concept of intelligence operations should provide for continuity of support even if communications are severely stressed or temporarily lost. An important component of survivability is redundancy in critical intelligence architectural components and capabilities.

(7) **Identify Key Personnel in the Area of Responsibility**. The Joint Force J2 should prepare/update a comprehensive list of points of contact (POC) throughout all echelons in theater (to include, but not limited to, intelligence personnel/teams, collection management personnel/teams, ISR asset owners, combined air operations center (CAOC) personnel, etc), and prepare to engage each element in dialogue through any applicable mode of communication, and creating an enduring relationship. This list should be disseminated throughout the theater to the lowest level, and incoming units should be provided these lists to assist them in developing new relationships. They in turn can update the list throughout their deployment cycle.

(8) **Provide Information in a Usable Format**. If real-time display is not available for all echelons, a static view of a comprehensive collection plan can be disseminated to all echelons that details national to tactical level collection activity and shows the synchronization (or potential synchronization) of assets across space and time. This is a time proven method of promoting shared situational awareness of collection assets and tasking.

(9) **Identify and Share Best Practices**. It should not be underestimated how critical it is for collection managers, analysts, and operators of ISR assets throughout all echelons to communicate, collaborate, and coordinate best practices throughout the deployment timeframe, not only when new/incoming units are coming into theater. This will enable effective planning for persistent surveillance missions and refine techniques.

5. **Joint Force Operations Staff's Responsibilities**

a. The J3 assists the commander in the discharge of assigned responsibility for the direction and control of operations, beginning with planning and follow-through until the commander's intent and end state have been achieved. In this capacity the J-3 plans, coordinates and integrates operations.

b. **Identify persistent surveillance missions**. During operations the J3 may determine that persistent surveillance is required in order to support the mission. The identified PS mission should be immediately coordinated with the J2 to ensure that the mission is supportable, and coordination of requirements, assets and information flow can begin.

c. **Conduct persistent surveillance missions**. Persistent surveillance missions require close coordination between operations and intelligence. The complexities involved requires operations to assess and prioritize other missions that may lose assets to persistent surveillance, as well as identify what units may be used as non-traditional collection assets and task those units accordingly.

d. **Assess persistent surveillance**. During the operation, the J3 should assess the collection being done in support of the mission, and provide feedback in order to make immediate adjustments to the collection strategy.

6. Joint Force J5 Responsibilities

The J5 assists the commander in long-range or future planning preparation of campaign and joint operational plans (OPLANs), and associated estimates of the situation. Due to the requirements to plan and coordinate for persistent surveillance missions, it is important that these missions be identified as early as possible. When, in the course of creating future plans, persistent surveillance requirements are identified, the task of coordinating with the J2 should begin immediately. After the mission, the J5 should use the results of the assessment of the persistent surveillance mission to improve and refine future planning.

7. Collaboration between Operations and Intelligence

"Timely fusion of all sources of information can only be accomplished through aggressive intelligence-operations teaming, a shared common operating picture of the environment, relevant military intelligence capabilities, and the effective employment of organic and supporting military intelligence assets."

"Military Intelligence Rebalancing"
Information Paper for 2010 Army Posture Statement

a. Intelligence must be synchronized with operations and plans in order to provide answers to intelligence requirements in time to influence the decisions they are intended to support. Intelligence synchronization requires that all intelligence sources and methods be applied in concert with commander's intent and end state. Commander's intent and end state requirements therefore constitute the principal driving force that dictates the timing and sequencing of intelligence operations.

b. Intelligence includes organizations, processes, and products, as well as the collection, processing, exploitation, analysis, and dissemination of information required by decision makers. Intelligence, however, is not an end in itself. For intelligence to have utility, it must focus on user defined requirements. Thus, an examination of whether or not persistent surveillance is effective or influential not only depends on the intelligence organizations, processes, and products, but must also consider how well it satisfied the user's requirements. This is discussed in detail in the section on assessment.

c. Intelligence provides the commander with a threat assessment based on an analysis of the full range of adversary capabilities, and a prediction of the adversary's likely intentions. With predictive, accurate, and relevant intelligence, commanders may gain the critical advantage of getting inside the adversary's decision-making cycle, improving insight into how the adversary will act or react.

    d. During collection planning, the intelligence staff coordinates closely with the operations staff in order to anticipate operational support requirements for the development and execution of adaptive collection plans. Accordingly, the collection requirements and asset status must be monitored and updated, and the collection plan synchronized. Active involvement of targeteers, analysts, and operations staff (J3) personnel in concert with the collection managers is critical to the success of persistent surveillance. Collection managers must ensure that the collection plan is synchronized with the OPLAN so that collection efforts are focused correctly across the critical time identified for persistent surveillance. Additionally, reconnaissance and surveillance operations must be integrated with other forms of intelligence collection operations, and coordinated with counterintelligence activities.

Intentionally Blank

CHAPTER III
PLANNING AND PREPARATION

1. Understand the Operational Environment

In planning any joint operation, to include persistent surveillance, it is essential to understand the operational environment, which includes conducting JIPOE, determining what the intended targets are through target development, and ensuring situational awareness for the commander.

a. **Joint Intelligence Preparation of the Operational Environment.** JIPOE is a key tool for conducting intelligence analysis and production.

(1) The purpose of JIPOE is to support the JFC by determining the adversary's probable intent, adversary key nodes and targets, and likely courses of action (COAs) for countering the overall friendly joint mission.[2]

(2) JIPOE is the analytical process used by joint intelligence organizations to produce intelligence estimates and other intelligence products in support of the JFC's decision-making process. It is a continuous process that involves four major steps:

(a) defining the operational environment

(b) describing the impact of the operational environment

(c) evaluating the adversary

(d) determining and describing adversary potential COAs, particularly the most likely and most dangerous COA.

(3) The JIPOE process assists in achieving information superiority by identifying adversary centers of gravity (COGs) and critical vulnerabilities (CV), focusing intelligence collection at the right time and place, and analyzing the impact of the operational environment on military operations.

(4) Once the desired conditions, effects, and impacts on the objectives have been identified; those special issues that require persistent surveillance in order to be resolved should be identified and processed accordingly.

(5) The development of the physical factors (area of operation, weather, culture, and infrastructure) and information factors (the collection, processing, and dissemination of information both physically and cognitively) will identify when and where to focus persistent surveillance.

For additional detailed information, see JP 2-01.3, Joint Intelligence Preparation of the Operational Environment.)

b. **Target Development**

(1) Targeting is the process of selecting and prioritizing targets, and matching the appropriate response to them, considering operational requirements and capabilities. A target is an entity or object considered for possible engagement or action. A target's importance is derived from its assessed relationship with planned operations to achieve the commander's objective(s) and the end state. The joint targeting cycle is an iterative process that is not time-constrained, and steps may occur concurrently, providing a helpful framework to describe the steps that must be satisfied to successfully conduct joint targeting. The joint targeting cycle consists of the following six phases:

(a) end state and commander's objectives

(b) target development and prioritization

(c) capabilities analysis

(d) commander's decision and force assignment

(e) mission planning and force execution

(f) assessment.

(2) As part of phase two of the joint targeting cycle, target development is interrelated with intelligence planning. JIPOE is an input to target development, and the intelligence staff of the supported commander will lead the target intelligence planning effort. Target intelligence is intelligence that portrays and locates the components of a target or target complex, and indicates its vulnerability and relative importance. It involves the analysis of facilities, systems, and nodes relative to the mission, objectives, and the capabilities at the JFC's disposal. It identifies and nominates specific COGs and HVTs that, if exploited in a systematic manner, will create the desired effects and support accomplishment of the commander's objectives. Target intelligence includes nominations for the no-strike list and restricted target list.

(3) Target Development consists of the following:

(a) The systematic examination of potential target systems and their components, individual targets, and even elements of targets to determine the type and duration of the action that must be exerted on each target to create an effect that is consistent with the commander's specific objectives.[3]

(b) Conducting a target system analysis (TSA), which is an all-source examination of potential targets to determine relevance to stated objectives, military importance, and priority of attack. It is an open-ended analytic process produced through the intelligence production process using national and theater validated requirements as a foundation. Typical products include nodal system analysis studies. TSA identifies critical components or nodes of a target system, which are used as the base line for target selection.

(c) Target vetting and validation determine whether a target remains a viable element of the target system, and whether it is a lawful target under the law of armed conflict and rules of engagement.

(d) Targets are nominated, through the proper channels, for approval. Targets are prioritized based on the JFC's guidance and intent.

(4) The target development process will help to identify centers of gravity and high value targets that will require persistent surveillance to prosecute. Persistent surveillance also may be required in order to positively identify targets for prosecution.

c. **Situational Awareness**

The commander must maintain a current, accurate picture of the operational environment. The more comprehensive the understanding, the better the commander's guidance and intent. Once key situations are identified, persistent surveillance helps develop that awareness by watching key areas or individuals to immediately identify those events that change the situation. The quicker a commander can update situational awareness, the quicker that commander can act.

2. **Key Considerations for Planning Persistent Surveillance Missions**

a. The following issues should be addressed in planning persistent surveillance missions:

(1) All units engaged within the combatant commander (CCDR)'s area of responsibility should conform to consistent procedures for managing assets and requirements in a complex environment. There will often be separate units requesting information, operating assets, and reviewing collected information. The roles and responsibilities of each unit need to be addressed, and guidance disseminated that addresses their responsibilities to each other.

(2) If there is concern that the lower echelons cannot manage all required assets and information requirements, the operational control of assets can take place at higher echelons, which have the manning and communications systems necessary to control multi-platform operations. However, the tactical control of the assets and overall mission need to remain at the requesting echelon, which is closest to the fight.

(3) The Commander must have a firm understanding of what organic assets are available for tasking, and also what is available at higher, lower, and adjacent commands. Proper planning for any persistent surveillance mission must take into account all the

available assets (both intelligence and operational assets, standard and non-standard), their capabilities, limitations, and coordination requirements.

(4) Understanding asset capabilities will help identify those assets best suited for the specific persistent surveillance mission. The planning team must also identify limitations that may need to be addressed by requesting additional assets or using non-traditional capabilities. Planning for inclusion of these assets must begin prior to an actual event.

(5) Persistent surveillance plans should consider some key questions about an operational or intelligence asset as cited in Figure III-1, below:

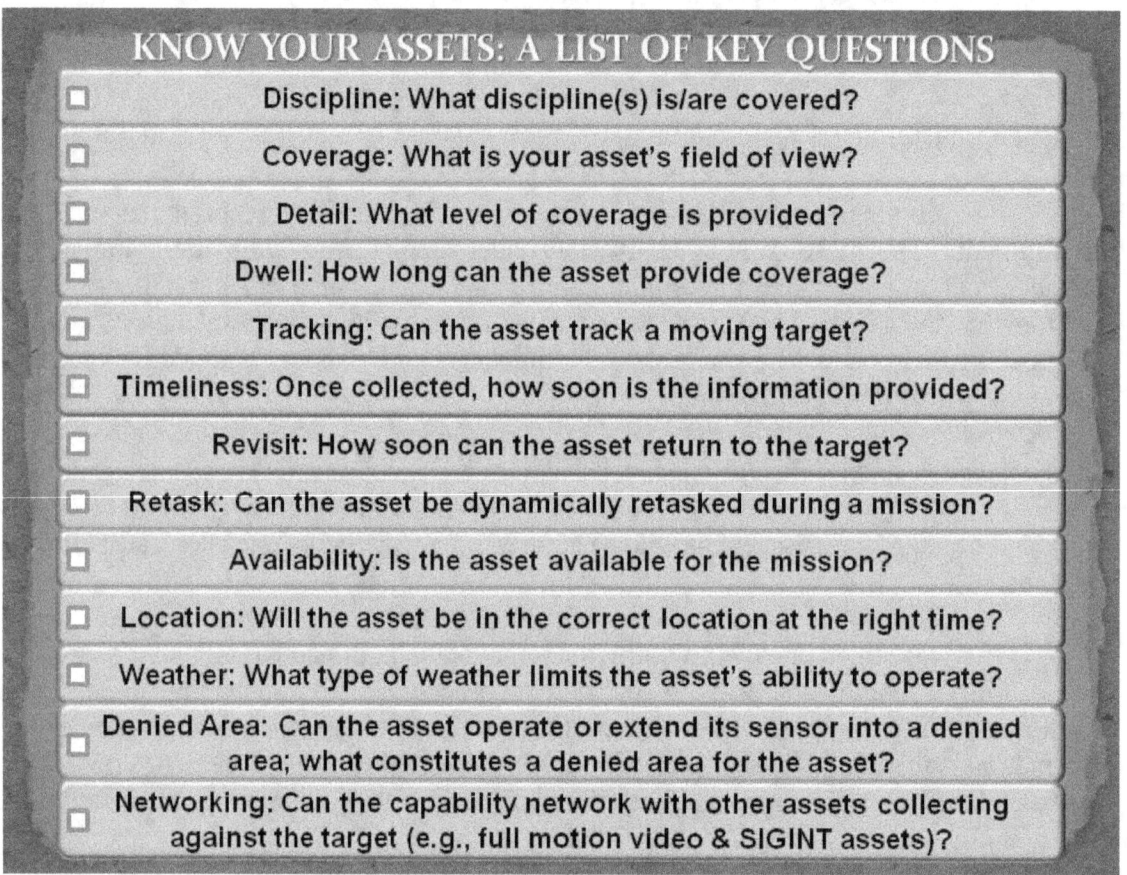

KNOW YOUR ASSETS: A LIST OF KEY QUESTIONS

- Discipline: What discipline(s) is/are covered?
- Coverage: What is your asset's field of view?
- Detail: What level of coverage is provided?
- Dwell: How long can the asset provide coverage?
- Tracking: Can the asset track a moving target?
- Timeliness: Once collected, how soon is the information provided?
- Revisit: How soon can the asset return to the target?
- Retask: Can the asset be dynamically retasked during a mission?
- Availability: Is the asset available for the mission?
- Location: Will the asset be in the correct location at the right time?
- Weather: What type of weather limits the asset's ability to operate?
- Denied Area: Can the asset operate or extend its sensor into a denied area; what constitutes a denied area for the asset?
- Networking: Can the capability network with other assets collecting against the target (e.g., full motion video & SIGINT assets)?

Figure III-1. Know Your Assets: A List of Key Questions

(6) The JTF should maintain situational awareness of the status, location, and capabilities of all assets that can be tasked to conduct persistent surveillance. Dwell time, responsiveness, and re-tasking ability are the most important requirements for any persistent surveillance asset, but all missions will have unique requirements for detail, coverage, or discipline.

(7) Each contingency should be covered by clearly understood tactics, techniques, and procedures that describe the actions to be taken, and what coordination needs to occur both before and after the event occurs. Planners, requestors, and asset

managers should be informed of the planned changes to collection assets, and the procedures used to cover unplanned events.

(8) Persistent surveillance missions happen in the context of a larger operation. Just as commanders need to be aware of what other assets are available, they need to be aware of the other requirements that exist. This will allow them to balance the intensive needs of a persistent surveillance mission with other important, but discrete requirements. Staff officers should brief their commanders on the overall impact to operations of the conduct of a persistent surveillance mission.

(9) All echelons must weigh the gains from persistent surveillance against the loss of collection on other requirements which results from conducting such manpower and asset intensive operations.

(10) Persistent surveillance planners must synchronize their efforts with supported military operations, and as much as possible, synchronize asset coverage to facilitate cross-cueing. Many collection assets are capable of providing valuable, but incomplete information for analysis or targeting. Cross-cueing provides the synergy to support real-time analytical cooperation and enables a comprehensive understanding of our adversaries. Collection assets may be scheduled as a package to support a certain persistent surveillance effect. As such, ISR planners must have the greatest visibility possible on all ISR operations in theater. An ISR synchronization matrix will provide ISR operators and end users the situational awareness of the where, when, what, and why for each ISR mission. ISR planners will coordinate with the JOC and collection operations managers for other forms of ISR in order to maximize synchronization and cross-cueing across the entire ISR enterprise.

(11) Collection planning may also include coordinated actions with component operations to influence the adversary and improve the chance of successful detection. For example, if joint forces strike nodes in a country's fiber optic communications network, the adversary may be forced to talk on collectible open-air means. Another example would be posturing ISR assets around a village prior to a known raid by friendly ground forces in an effort to "see" and "hear" how the enemy reacts for targeting opportunities or patterns of life development. The trend in modern warfare is to fight for information, instead of with information. This requires extensive coordination between ISR and operations planners.

3. Integration of the Joint Operation Planning, Intelligence, and Targeting Processes

a. The processes for joint operation planning, targeting, and intelligence are distinct cycles that involve different steps conducted at different times by different staff members. Each, however, has an impact on the development of persistent surveillance, and they must be integrated and synchronized in order for persistent surveillance to be effective.

b.   Commanders and planning staffs have to coordinate their efforts, and keep those using the other cycles informed of issues that relate to persistent surveillance.   For example, A COG identified during JIPOE can be processed in the targeting cycle for development of specific HVT related to that COG. The intelligence cycle then identifies indicators for the HVT, all of which would be a part of a persistent surveillance mission that might not have been identified if each cycle was operated independently.   Only through coordination will the many requirements to properly identify, plan, and execute a persistent surveillance mission be answered.

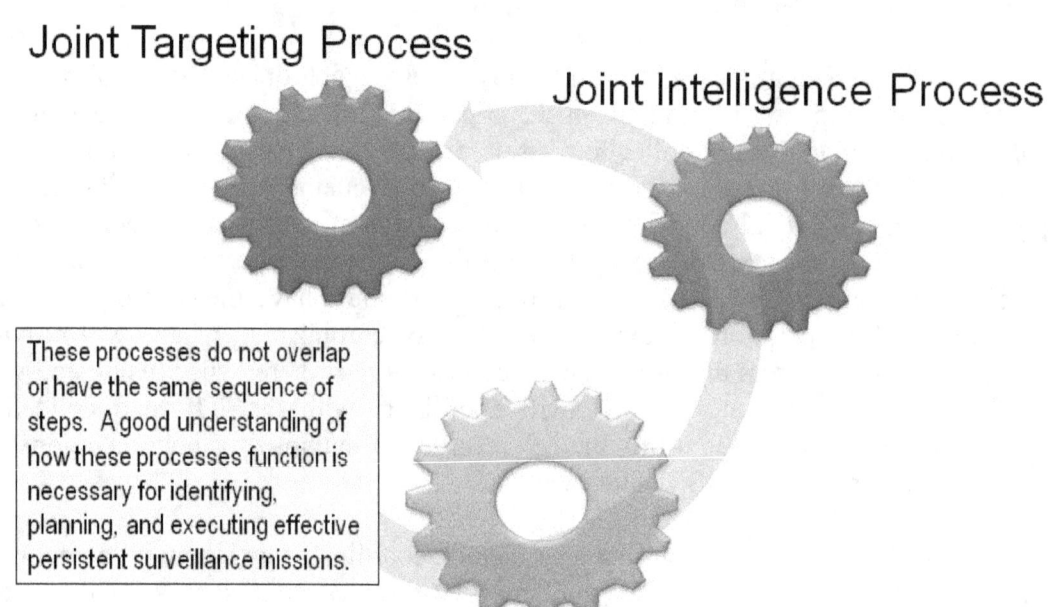

JOINT PROCESSES

Joint Targeting Process

Joint Intelligence Process

These processes do not overlap or have the same sequence of steps. A good understanding of how these processes function is necessary for identifying, planning, and executing effective persistent surveillance missions.

Joint Operation Planning Process

Figure III-2. Joint Processes

CHAPTER IV
MANAGING REQUIREMENTS AND TASKING

1. **Request for Information**

a. **The process of managing requirements and tasking assets for collection begins with the commander's mission, designated end state and guidance on achieving that objective.** Reliable information is required in order to conduct effective operations. Because there is a possibility that the required information has already been collected and is available in intelligence databases, submitting a request for information (RFI) is a recommended place to start.

KEY TERM – REQUEST FOR INFORMATION

"A specific time-sensitive ad hoc requirement for information or intelligence products, and is distinct from standing requirements or scheduled intelligence production. An RFI can be initiated at any level of command, and will be validated in accordance with the combatant command's procedures."

JP 1-02, Department of Defense Dictionary of Military and Associated Terms

---

b. An RFI that is received by the collection management section is first reviewed by the collection requirements manager. The collection requirements manager will review the RFI for completeness. Completeness entails an understanding of the following questions:

(1) What is the requested information?

(2) Does the requested information already exist?

(3) Why is this information requested?—a justification will explain the need for the information

(4) What is the best means of obtaining the information if it is not already available?

(5) When is the information required?

(6) When is the latest time the information is of value?

(7) In what format is the information required?

(8) Are there any special instructions for the RFI?

(9) What intelligence discipline or disciplines are best suited to answer the request?

c. After reviewing all of the above criteria, the collection requirements manager will validate the RFI for collection and recommend a priority based on supporting the commander's mission, intent, and decisions. Lastly, the collection requirements manager will look at the possibility of consolidating the RFI with other requests into a single collection requirement. If the RFI is not validated by the collection requirements manager for collection, it is sent back to the requestor with an explanation why the request was disapproved.

d. A validated RFI is forwarded for action to the collection operations manager as a collection requirement. An RFI for persistent surveillance should clearly state what it is, who it is for, and what it is intended to accomplish. Tracking requirements through the entire process, to include feedback from the user of the information, is a fundamental element of successful requirements management, which aids in successful collection and production of intelligence.

e. Once intelligence requirements and information requirements are established, intelligence personnel review existing intelligence databases for answers to the requirements. An RFI will lead to a production requirement if the request can be answered with information on hand. Units have the option of forwarding an RFI to the next higher headquarters for processing if it cannot be satisfied internally or through informal analyst coordination.

2. Collection Requirements Management

a. If the intelligence does not already exist, the RFI should be issued as a new collection requirement and the unit's intelligence section should initiate the development or revision of the collection plan.

KEY TERM – COLLECTION REQUIREMENT

"**An intelligence need considered in the allocation of intelligence resources. Within the Department of Defense, these collection requirements fulfill the essential elements of information and other intelligence needs of a commander, or an agency.**"

JP 1-02, Department of Defense Dictionary of Military and Associated Terms

---

b. Collection requirements management ensures that all collection requirements are appropriately documented, prioritized, and linked to the commander's decision points, key nodes, and PIRs/essential elements of information (EEIs). Collection requirements managers synchronize the timing of collection with the operational scheme of maneuver, and then with the other intelligence operations – processing and exploitation, analysis and production, and dissemination. Commanders drive the intelligence process through their guidance, intent, and end state thus providing the collection manager with sufficiently detailed information requirements to allow the formulation of collection requirements, and the allocation and apportionment of collection assets in support of those requirements. This process culminates in preparation and/or revision of the command's intelligence collection plan, which tasks or submits intelligence requirements to the appropriate internal and external supporting intelligence organizations and agencies.

c. **Theater Level Management**. Management and validation of collection requirement requests for a theater reside at the CCDR level. The validation process parallels that for RFIs and is responsive to operational requirements. The theater intelligence operations center validates and submits collection requirements to the Defense Intelligence Agency if requirements cannot be satisfied by organic or subordinate assets.[4]

(1) The subordinate joint force J-2 validates collection requirements and submits requests for additional collection resources to the combatant command J-2. The combatant command J-2 validates or modifies standing collection requirements submitted by subordinate joint force or component commands.

(2) The joint intelligence center tracks the status of research, validation, submission and satisfaction of all collection requests received. At the JFC's discretion, a joint collection management board (JCMB) may be formed to serve as a joint forum for the management of collection requirements and the coordination of collection operations.

(3) The JCMB is chaired by the J-2, or his representative, and should include J-3 and component representatives. If formed, the JCMB receives collection target nominations from the components and the JFC's staff, validates and prioritizes these requirements into a joint integrated prioritized collection list (JIPCL), and recommends the apportionment of organic ISR assets to meet JIPCL requirements.

3. Collection Operations Management

Collection operations management (COM) involves the direction, scheduling, and control of specific collection platforms, sensors, and HUMINT sources and alignment of processing, exploitation, and reporting resources with planned collection. COM duties include development and coordination of sensor employment guidance that helps shape collection plans and strategies, and ensures the best allocation of intelligence requirements to collection resources. Collections activities are continuous, and include monitoring the overall satisfaction of these requirements and assessing the effectiveness of the collection strategy to satisfy the original and evolving intelligence needs. Collected data is distributed via appropriately classified networks/links to processing and exploitation elements.

4. Planned Collection Task

A planned collection task is one that is derived from the deliberate planning process. This process is not inherently specific to persistent surveillance. Appendix A provides guidance and recommendations for a persistent surveillance planner. Adhering to the preparation and planning considerations described in the preceding chapter will support execution of the recommended tasks and consequently, successful planning for persistent surveillance missions.

5. Ad Hoc Collection Request

a. An Ad hoc requirement is a collection requirement (not disruptive nor immediate) received outside the normal/deliberate ISR operations planning cycle (i.e., after the Reconnaissance, Surveillance, and Target Acquisition (RSTA) annex has been pushed for execution) and requires collection during the current air tasking order (ATO) day. Proper coordination procedures must be established early and communicated through the chain of command. The RSTA annex, provided on a daily basis, will serve as the primary reference for requirements and tasking.

b. Each theater of operations may have a different process for submitting requirements. Non-critical Ad hoc requirements are likely submitted by email or through chat by using a standard form. However, dynamic ad hoc collection requests (critical and time-sensitive) are submitted through the most expeditious means possible, most often by voice via phone, or via Internet Relay Chat (IRC).

SOMETHING TO THINK ABOUT

"Comprehensive coordination between operations and intelligence from the inception of major operations ensures that critical collection requirements are as well forecast and resourced as possible. However, it is important to note that deliberate planning for ISR support of counterinsurgency warfare does not alter the fact that more immediate and critical requirements emerge and continually evolve. In fact, the ability to retask assets quickly is an important aspect of exploiting operational and strategic opportunities that present themselves and are in line with the commander's intent and standing ISR priorities."

Flynn, Juergens, & Cantrell

---

6. Dynamic Ad hoc Collection Re-tasking

a. Dynamic re-tasking occurs when a requester identifies a time-sensitive need after the allocation of ISR assets, causing some level of disruption to the approved collection plan. This may be due to an opportunity to track a time sensitive target or some other indicator in which there may be a small window for successful surveillance. The identified surveillance target must meet the priority collection requirements previously established by commander's guidance. Because the available collection platforms were already allocated, the asset with the best sensor configuration to successfully accomplish the new tasking may not be available. Thus, commanders should carefully consider the advantages and disadvantages of initiating dynamic re-taskings before deciding to re-task assets executing a pre-planned mission. This is particularly true of persistent surveillance missions due to their extended duration and near constant use of surveillance assets. The parameters under which dynamic re-tasking takes place are a part of ISR strategy development, and are documented in the Joint Air Operations Plan and RSTA Annex.

b. **Dynamic re-tasking of assets must be a planning consideration for all persistent surveillance missions.** During the course of the operation, persistent surveillance planners will also need to consider adding additional assets and/or removing assets during the mission as required. Any change in asset availability, during the mission, is a chance for the surveillance operation to fail. A mismatched asset/sensor capability against a target's signatures and observables or a mismanaged hand-off of collection could cause the loss of collection on the target. The complexity of a persistent surveillance mission may require such constant and focused management that without proper understanding of commander's intent, support to other operations and collection opportunities are missed by the staff.

    c. In order to make re-tasking decisions during ongoing persistent surveillance missions, the unit that is handling the persistent surveillance mission, the unit requesting the new requirement and the asset managers need to be in agreement. Issues that impact this decision-making are: how do the new requirements compare to the overall CCIRs; how long would an asset be removed from the ongoing persistent surveillance mission; and what other assets are available that could give similar, if degraded, coverage (the "next best" answer).

    d. Re-tasking operations can occur as the result of four scenarios, as depicted in Figure IV-1 and listed below, each with its own causes and effects. While the below terms may not be standardized across the Department of Defense (DOD), all commands will have to prepare for the eventualities identified below in order to conduct persistent surveillance missions.

    (1) **Tipping** is the use of one intelligence discipline, asset, or sensor type to cross-cue or initiate collection by another sensor.

    (2) **Hand-Off**. One asset stops collection against a specific target as another asset begins collection on the same target. This can either be a planned or unplanned event. In a planned event, the first collection asset comes off station at a predetermined time and is replaced as scheduled by a second collection asset. A more difficult situation to manage is an unplanned handoff. Both situations require communication and coordination between the mission complete asset, the asset assuming the mission, and the controlling headquarters until the new asset has positive control of the target. The coordination required increases when a target of interest crosses unit boundaries and handoff must be conducted by adjacent units.

    (3) **Cross-Cueing**. Additional information is required concerning a collection opportunity. A second asset is tasked that can provide greater visibility and validity of the target to confirm assumptions or provide additional detail. This could be a planned event, as the need for additional information can be recognized early in the planning phases of a persistent surveillance mission, with assets already identified for cross cueing. Both assets usually continue to monitor the target after the cross-cueing is completed.

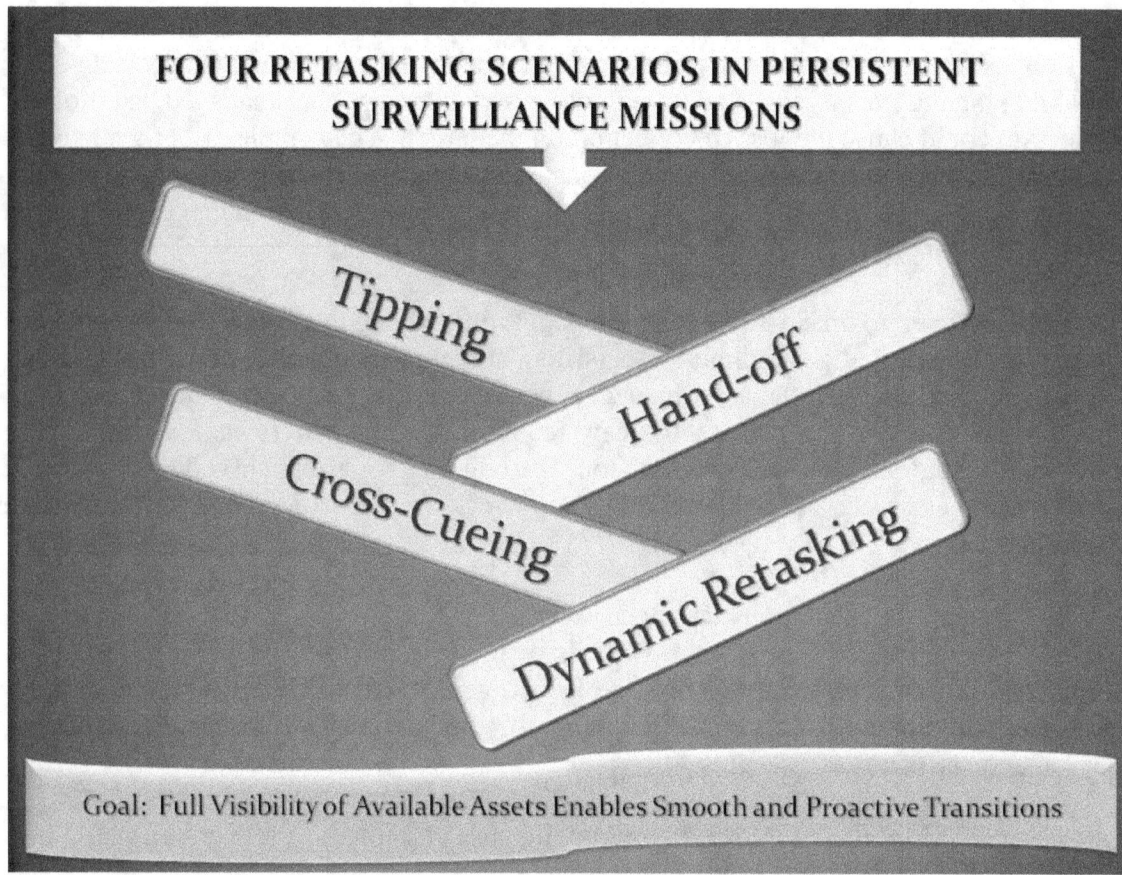

Figure IV-1. Four Re-tasking Scenarios in Persistent Surveillance Missions

(4) **Dynamic Re-tasking** occurs when the requester identifies a time sensitive need after ISR assets have already been tasked. It is an unplanned yet possibly anticipated event which occurs at an unknown time. Coordination in this case should include plans to satisfy collection requirements that may be pre-empted by the dynamic tasking, or at a minimum, informing units that their collection requirements will not be collected as scheduled because of high priority tasking. These operations must be closely managed by operations and coordinated with intelligence to determine the intelligence gain / loss. Commander's intent and priorities are critical aspects of that decision making process.

e.   Each of the above contingencies should be covered by clearly understood TTPs that describe the actions to be taken, and what coordination needs to occur both before and after the event occurs. Planners, requestors, and asset managers should be informed of the planned changes to collection assets, and the procedures used to cover unplanned events.

f.   Persistent surveillance missions occur in the context of larger operations. Just as commanders need to be aware of what other assets are available, they need to be aware of the other requirements that exist. This will allow them to balance the intensive needs of a persistent surveillance mission with other important, critical requirements. Staff officers should brief their commanders on the overall impact to operations of the conduct of a persistent surveillance mission.

g.   All echelons must weigh the gains from persistent surveillance against the loss of collection on other requirements that result from conducting such manpower and asset intensive operations. Re-tasking for time sensitive targets and emerging requirements have an impact on existing collection operations. The prioritization of requirements and visibility across echelons and intelligence disciplines will greatly decrease the chance of diverting an asset from a critical collection operation.

7.   Collaboration and Synchronization

The goal at every echelon, and across all services within the joint force, must be to actively share operational awareness concerning collection assets and requirements. This requires a detailed understanding of the command and control (C2) and collection management architecture available in theater so that asset owners and requirements managers can determine the best way to disseminate relevant data up, down and across the chain of command. It cannot be stressed enough how important it is to have a collection strategy that is equally synchronized (Figure IV-2) and visible to all echelons operating within a joint force in theater.

SOMETHING TO THINK ABOUT

A Spiral One After Action Report, ISR Analysis, conducted by the Integrated Demonstration and Experiment Cooperative Research and Development Agreement in December 2007 suggested that persistent surveillance was achieved when the collection and production activities of the ISR mission package were synchronized, and the results of these activities were fully integrated with the decisive points of the military operation. Synchronization was achieved with effective communication and collaboration between the on-scene ISR mission coordinator and key participants of the ISR mission package.

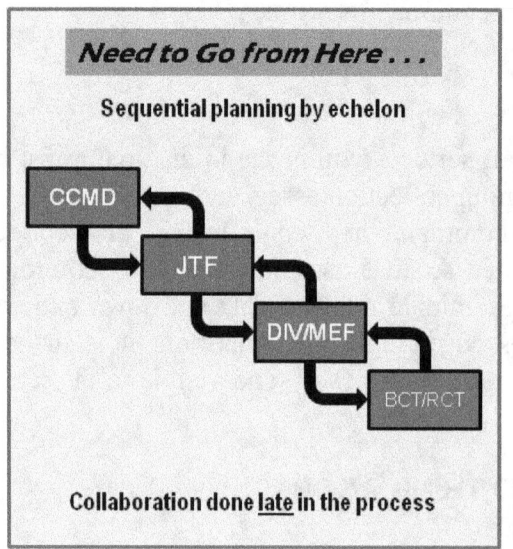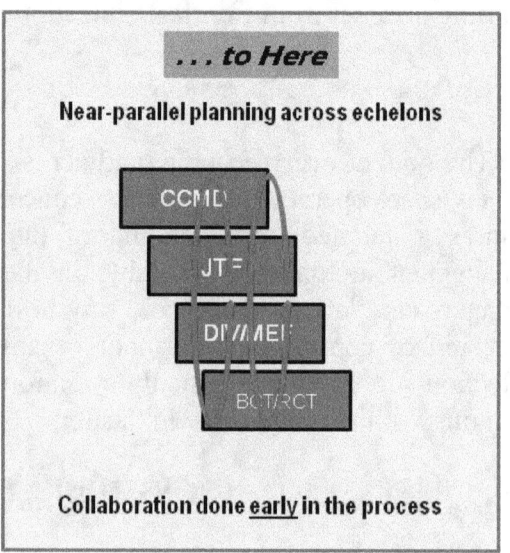

INTELLIGENCE, SURVEILLANCE, AND RECONNAISSANCE PLANNING
Collaboration and Synchronization

Need to Go from Here . . .

Sequential planning by echelon

CCMD

JTF

DIV/MEF

BCT/RCT

Collaboration done <u>late</u> in the process

. . . to Here

Near-parallel planning across echelons

CCMD

JTF

DIV/MEF

BCT/RCT

Collaboration done <u>early</u> in the process

Figure IV-2. Intelligence, Surveillance, and Reconnaissance Planning

CHAPTER V
VISUALIZATION AND TRACKING

1. Introduction

a. The doctrinal definition of ISR visualization is as follows: "The capability to graphically display the current and future locations of intelligence, surveillance, and reconnaissance sensors, their projected platform tracks, vulnerability to threat capabilities and meteorological and oceanographic phenomena, fields of regard, tasked collection targets, and products to provide a basis for dynamic re-tasking and time-sensitive decision making" (JP 1-02). In the context of this handbook, "visualization" in general refers to geospatial, graphical, or textual aids that provide information required for shared operational awareness of blue force (U.S. and coalition) requirements and activities (historical, current, and planned) to facilitate the efficient planning and direction of collection operations. Collection requirements management and collection operations management, while simple in concept, are complex procedures that require significant cross-organizational and cross-security domain coordination to effectively meet the commander's information needs. Given their complexity, there exists no single tool that provides comprehensive (national to tactical to coalition) visualization capabilities in support of these procedures.

b. **Asset Visibility**

(1) Although not a point of emphasis in doctrine, asset visibility is cited at the tactical level and further validated through the operational level and by the CCDRs as being essential to achieving enhanced persistent surveillance. From the operational to tactical levels, planners are not able to easily see which collection assets are conducting missions, their tasking, and their future availability.

(2) Collection planning requires knowledge of asset status for all assets at all echelons that may be brought to bear on a collection manager's tasks. Shared knowledge of historical, current, and planned collection asset status across national, theater, operational, tactical, coalition, and other organizational boundaries enhances collaboration between echelons, resulting in enhanced processes, particularly for the dynamic re-tasking of collection assets to meet emergent requirements.

c. **Collection Requirements Visibility**

(1) Another key enabler for persistent surveillance mission planning is the need for collection managers to view all collection requirements submitted by adjacent units and higher headquarters. This should include submitted RFIs, collection requirements validated for tasking, collection requirements currently tasked for collection, and closed collection requirements. Visibility is required for requirements at all echelons to allow planners to combine and deconflict requirements and make best use of the available collection capacity.

(2) Visibility of collection requirements across echelons will be a significant step forward in conducting persistent surveillance missions, but there are implied and adjunct capabilities which provide further benefits. This includes operations enabled by improved visibility. Requirement traceability from the originator, through the planning and collection processes, and then tracking the collected information back to the user will allow support assessment of the effectiveness of collection and improve the timeliness of the intelligence support to operations.

(3) Visibility of all requirements will allow collection managers to detect unintentional redundant collection and coordinate dissemination of existing products, freeing up capability. It also allows leveraging other echelons for tipping and cross-cuing when they have similar issues but different capabilities.

d. **Intelligence Data Visibility**

Having broad visibility of all intelligence data and products provides benefits beyond the scope of persistent surveillance. It is a long standing goal of collection managers and intelligence directors. Enhanced intelligence data visibility contributes to better informing planning and target development. Also by supporting better data correlation, visibility enhances cross-cueing opportunities. Enhanced intelligence data visibility can also reduce collection tasking by satisfying requirements with information that has already been collected.

e. While existing tools enable cross-echelon visualization to a degree, i.e. from the national to JTF-level, a comprehensive national to tactical visualization capability does not rest on a single tool. Rather, the ability to achieve national to tactical visualization requires a mindset on the part of collection managers to actively and aggressively seek and share the data and information required for efficient collection management synergy across echelons.

2. Common Operational Picture

a. A method to achieve visualization is the creation of an ISR common operational picture/user defined operational picture (COP/UDOP) that integrates separate ISR collection strategies into a comprehensive collection plan from the national to tactical level (Figures V-1 and V-2). The COP is defined in doctrine as, "a single identical display of relevant information shared by more than one command." The UDOP is a pre-doctrinal term that can be defined as the practice of creating and posting data according to net-centric information sharing standards that supports the visibility and accessibility of data in any number of visualization tools. This allows users to tailor their operational picture to meet local needs while also allowing two or more organizations to fuse, visualize, and analyze common information when needed. The COP/UDOP is useful beyond DOD to include all available players in the operating environment, such as other government agencies and coalition partners.[5]

b. Such a capability would provide operational awareness across echelons and achieve the following:

(1) Integrate ISR capabilities at all levels for a shared understanding

(2) Provide visibility of collection assets status and taskings (historical, current, and planned)

(3) Provide status of open and closed collection requirements

(4) Facilitate collaboration for both deliberate and dynamic planning

(5) Assist with anticipation of required decisions during current operations

(6) Support decision-making in time critical situations.

c. The following figure depicts how:

(1) Visualization through an ISR COP/UDOP can empower both the deliberate and dynamic collection planning processes.

(2) Planning and decision-making, regardless of echelon is a linear activity and the shared awareness provided by the ISR COP/UDOP, which relies on non-linear activities, will facilitate staff actions and recommendations to the commander.

d. Today's threat is not regional but global, mobile, and intertwined with civil and even commercial infrastructures. Persistent surveillance must be leveraged to meet our security requirements, by employing a shared COP/UDOP that supports military members with relevant, actionable data. Mechanisms and technologies also must be developed to allow broader access to data within a COP/UDOP from non-DOD and non-US elements based on the mission. A multinational-capable, tailorable COP/UDOP would foster global agility and coherent actions on the part of coalition forces.

c. For a COP/UDOP to be of use for persistent surveillance missions, it should contain the following information:

(1) **Blue and Green Forces** – Those operational units assigned to and maneuvering in the Commander's AO. This should also include host-nation units.

(2) **Red Forces** – Identified adversary forces, persons and locations identified as existing in the AO.

(3) **White Forces** – Critical individuals and locations associated with the local population and culture in the AO.

(4) **Collection Assets** – Intelligence forces assigned to and operating in the AO.

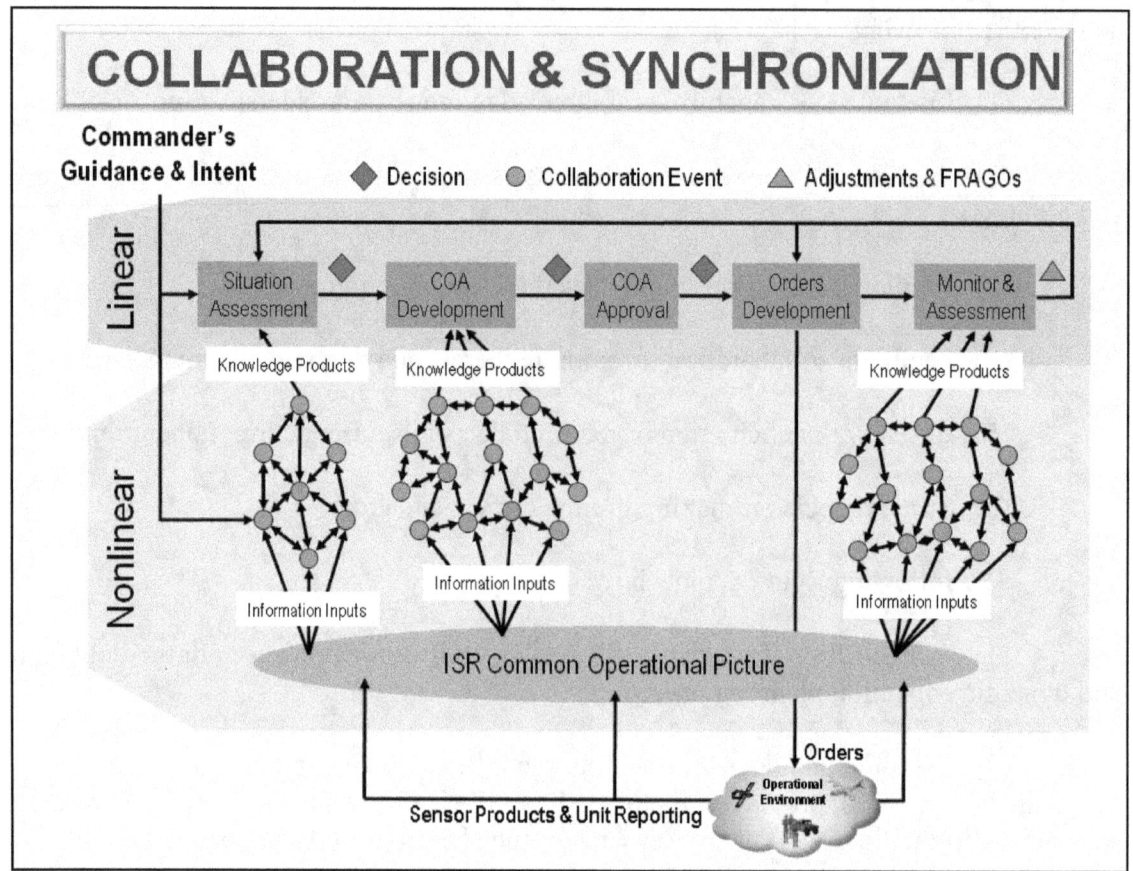

Figure V-1. Collaboration and Synchronization

(5) **Past, Current, and Planned Collection Operations**. Visibility of collection assets currently conducting missions, their assigned requirements, and sensor field of view is critical. This should include projected tracks of overhead/airborne collectors and ground locations of fixed collection assets. It would be incredibly useful to visualize historical as well as planned operations alongside those occurring in the present time.

Figure V-2. Common Operational Picture: Visualization and Tracking Recommendations

f. Having all the above information presented in a coherent manner allows commanders to derive knowledge from the multiple information feeds available. Unfortunately, lower echelons may only have access to a common tactical picture due to bandwidth or system limitations.

DID YOU KNOW?

The Joint Forces Command study on the collaborative information environment (CIE) found that collaboration capabilities allowed users to tailor COP displays yet maintain common, relevant aspects of the operational picture. The study also found that a real-time environment significantly increases the COP's value if the user can define and dynamically tailor the views. The key word is "if." We must transition to a COP with a dynamic tailoring capability to support real-time operating requirements and future planning requirements.

3. **Collection Asset Baseline**

a. The collection asset baseline (CAB) is a comprehensive, common and readily adaptable view of the available collection capabilities in a given theater of operations. Having a one-stop location in a standardized format for all assets (national/theater to tactical level/battalion) and their tasking, collection, processing, exploitation and dissemination (TCPED) requirements is a critical requirement for planning persistent surveillance missions (Figure V-3).

b. All echelons must define, establish, and maintain an operational view that enables understanding of the collection assets that may be available at all echelons, how these assets are tasked, how requirements for these assets are tracked, and how the intelligence collected is disseminated. For deploying units, this will require significant investment in researching the theater of operations they will deploy to and, if relieving a unit, close coordination with that unit to leverage the best practices they have developed for visualization and tracking. **The benefits of this approach to enabling PS collection missions are substantial, and this approach is consistent with Joint Collection Management best practices and the Army's ISR Synchronization doctrine.**

(1) For deliberate planning, asset and requirements visualization and tracking across all echelons enables more efficient use of assets (by eliminating unintended redundancies and allowing for consolidation of missions) and facilitates risk mitigation by providing planners a more robust framework for meeting priority collection requirements that compete with PS missions.

(2) For ad hoc and dynamic situations, development of the visualization and tracking operational architecture view will enable collection managers at all echelons to rapidly determine what assets may be applied to their PS requirements and provides them understanding of how to task these assets.

c. All echelons must also determine, enforce, and disseminate the means by which they will expose information on their collection assets and requirements. It is understood this approach is problematic for units at lower echelons. Concerns may exist about the manpower required to maintain this data, communications methods, and the possibility of higher headquarters tasking of tactical collection assets. **While these are valid issues, the benefits of asset and collection requirements visibility and tracking across echelons and coalition boundaries outweigh the potential risks.**

d. For higher echelons, such as the CAOC, the information on asset capabilities, status, and planned operations may be readily available and the process for posting and updating that data typically follows a well established procedure that varies little over time. Commands at all levels, though, must take a similar approach, flowing information about asset capabilities, readiness, and tasking up, down, and across the chain of command so that all units and commands involved in the AO understand the collections environment to ensure the most efficient use of all available assets.

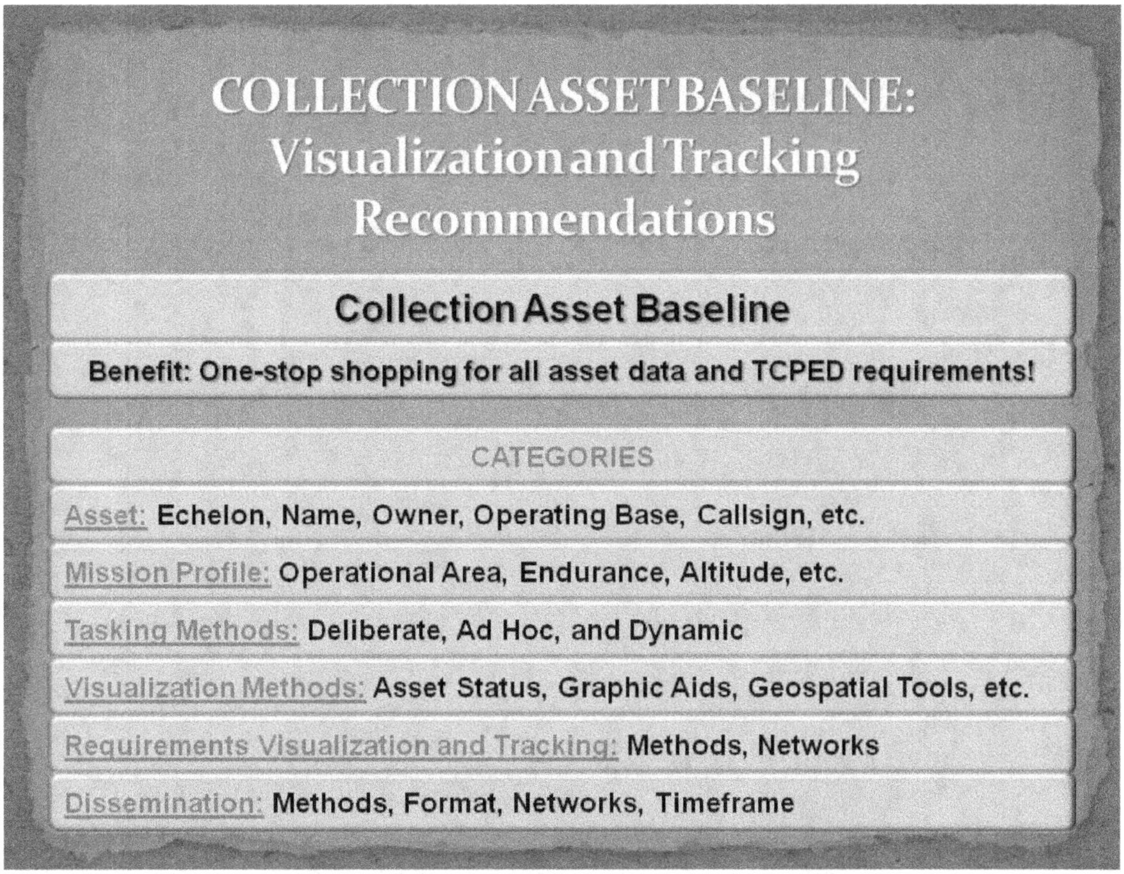

COLLECTION ASSET BASELINE: Visualization and Tracking Recommendations

Collection Asset Baseline

Benefit: One-stop shopping for all asset data and TCPED requirements!

CATEGORIES

Asset: Echelon, Name, Owner, Operating Base, Callsign, etc.

Mission Profile: Operational Area, Endurance, Altitude, etc.

Tasking Methods: Deliberate, Ad Hoc, and Dynamic

Visualization Methods: Asset Status, Graphic Aids, Geospatial Tools, etc.

Requirements Visualization and Tracking: Methods, Networks

Dissemination: Methods, Format, Networks, Timeframe

Figure V-3. The Collection Asset Baseline: Visualization and Tracking Recommendations

e.   The spreadsheet is organized with fields for asset information and TCPED requirements along the top row and an ordered list of assets ranging from national to battalion levels along the left-hand column. Graphic examples are found in Appendix B along with a notional example of a collection asset at brigade level. To standardize the spreadsheet, the following list represents the fields found within the top row of the spreadsheet.

    (1) **Asset Data:**

        (a) Echelon

        (b) Tasking Authority

        (c) Asset

        (d) Capabilities

        (e) Asset Owner

        (f) Operating Base

       (g) Call sign.

    (2) **Mission Profile:**

       (a) Supporting (which unit)

       (b) Operational Area (OPAREA)/Tracks/Field of View (FOV)

       (c) Mission Endurance

       (d) Flight Level

       (e) Named Areas of Interest (NAIs).

    (3) **Tasking Methods:**

       (a) Deliberate Planning Process

       (b) Deliberate Planning Network

       (c) Deliberate Planning Timeline

       (d) Ad Hoc/Dynamic Process

       (e) Ad Hoc/Dynamic Process Network

       (f) Ad Hoc/Dynamic Process Timeline.

    (4) **Asset Visualization Methods:**

       (a) Status/Readiness

       (b) Textual/Graphic

       (c) Geospatial.

    (5) **Requirements:**

       (a) Tracking Method

       (b) Network.

    (6) **Processing, Exploitation, and Dissemination (PED):**

       (a) Sensor Data-In Network

(b) Sensor Data-Out Network

(c) Raw Sensor Data Format

(d) Primary PED Node

(e) Secondary PED Node

(f) Exploitation Product(s)

(g) Exploited Product Format(s)

(h) Exploited Product Location(s)

(i) Network(s)

(j) Initial Report Timeframe

(k) 1st Phase Report Timeframe

(l) 2nd Phase Report Timeframe

(m) 3rd Phase Report Timeframe.

Intentionally Blank

CHAPTER VI
ASSESSMENT OF PERSISTENT SURVEILLANCE MISSIONS

1. **Assessment Defined**

a. Assessment as defined in joint doctrine is "a continuous process that measures the overall effectiveness of employing joint force capabilities during military operations."[6] Assessment of collection missions will use measures of performance (MOP) and measures of effectiveness (MOE).

(1) MOP is used to measure accomplishment of the ISR task. The result of MOP should answer the following questions:

(a) Did the collection mission take place?

(b) Did the collection mission obtain EEIs linked to the collection requirement?

(c) Did the collection mission gather the desired information (e.g., did the collection occur against the right target(s) at the right time)?

(2) The results of an MOE should assess whether a collection mission sufficiently answered the essential elements of information of a collection requirement. MOEs are used to assess changes in the operational environment and adversary behavior MOEs should be used to determine how sufficiently the commander's PIRs were satisfied, and by extension update his situational understanding, and support his decision-making.

b. Assessments for collection activities supporting operations are continuous. They begin with a mission analysis to determine the best suited ISR strategy. The overarching goal of the assessment process is to ensure that the commander is provided timely information necessary for him to make decisions. During execution, the operations and intelligence officers monitoring current operations will assess the effectiveness of ongoing collection activities toward accomplishing ISR tasks by obtaining the necessary information to support decision-making. The assessment actions taken during execution will allow commanders to:

(1) Adjust the collection plan and mix of ISR assets as required

(2) Direct dynamic re-tasking of assets

(3) Make other critical decisions to ensure the collection plan for current and future operations remains aligned with the commander's mission, intent, and desired end state.

c. Persistent surveillance assessment should consider the following:

(1) Was sufficient planning accomplished that focused on achieving the collection outcome?

(2) Were the collection assets tasked appropriate for the collection requirement to answer EEIs?

(3) Was sufficient time allocated for the collection requirement to ensure the ISR task was successful?

(4) Was the information collected within the time required to support a decision point?

d. Determining MOP is rather straightforward and quantitative; determining MOE is qualitative and can be challenging. The need to determine MOE underscores the importance of the human element in persistent surveillance.

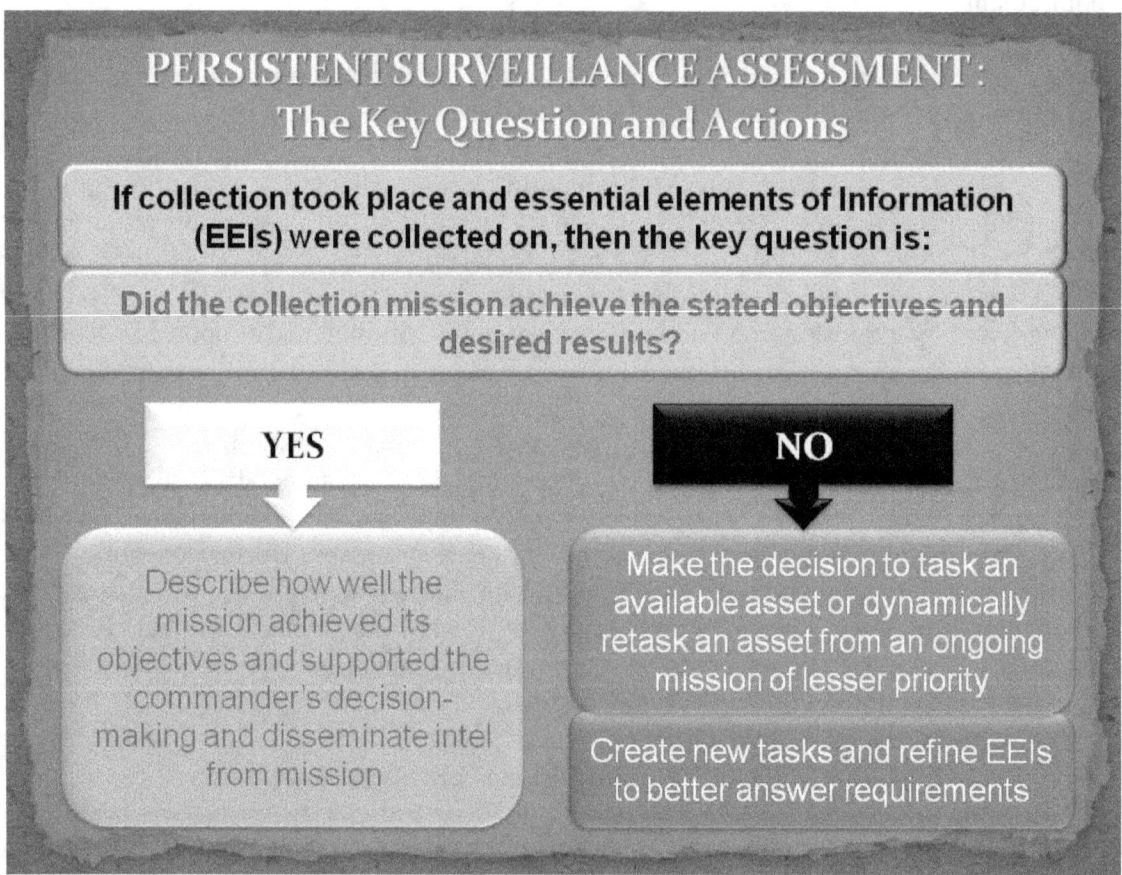

Figure VI-1. Persistent Surveillance Assessment: The Key Question and Actions

e. MOPs address the issues of "what sensor," "where" and "when" as relates to a specific collection requirement. When assessing the MOP for an ISR task, a determination is made whether the collection occurred, if the intended EEIs were collected on, and if the collection gathered the desired information. For example, was the target collected against with the desired sensor, at the desired location, and for the desired amount of time resulting in answers for the EEIs? MOEs address the issue of "how well" the collection supported decision making. The MOE is determined by addressing the question of whether the ISR task provided the commander with the information required to make a timely decision. If the answer to the MOE is no, then it becomes necessary to re-task collection to answer the collection requirement. It may become necessary, if the collection requirement is related to time sensitive decision-making, to dynamically re-task a collection asset from an ongoing ISR mission. The operations and intelligence officers monitoring current operations will propose a recommendation to the commander for a dynamic re-tasking and outline the intelligence, gain and loss likely to result from the re-tasking.

   f. Use the following (also illustrated in Figure VI-2) persistent surveillance terminology and definitions to guide the assessment process:

   (1) **PS Operational Intent**. Operational intent describes how PS missions will support achieving operational objectives and attaining the desired military end state. The PS operational intent is designed to focus PS missions on specific activities, e.g. find, fix, and identify (F2I), target tracking, change detection or determining level or type of activity, and provide prioritization guidance of PS missions in relation to other ISR missions.

   (2) **PS Objective**. PS objectives are goals which enable achievement of operational objectives. The PS objectives are a fusion of the PS mission, derived from the desired military end state, and the commander's guidance and intent for PS missions. PS objectives are centrally planned and de-centrally executed. PS objectives provide the "what" and "why" for PS mission planners and forces engaged in PS operations, as well as offer a mechanism on how to prioritize PS operations with other military operations.

   (3) **PS Desired Effect**. The PS desired effect represents the desired end state for the PS mission and how it supports operations. The PS desired effect answers the basic question: "At the end of this PS mission, will the commander possess the information he desires to inform his decision-making?" For example, "In order to approve the employment of lethal weapons, the commander desires confirmation that terrorist X is at known bomb making facility at location Y."

   (4) **PS Task**. PS tasks are actions that will create the PS desired effects and achieve the PS objectives. PS tasks provide direction on how specific intelligence disciplines and collection assets will support the creation of PS desired effects and achievement of PS objectives.

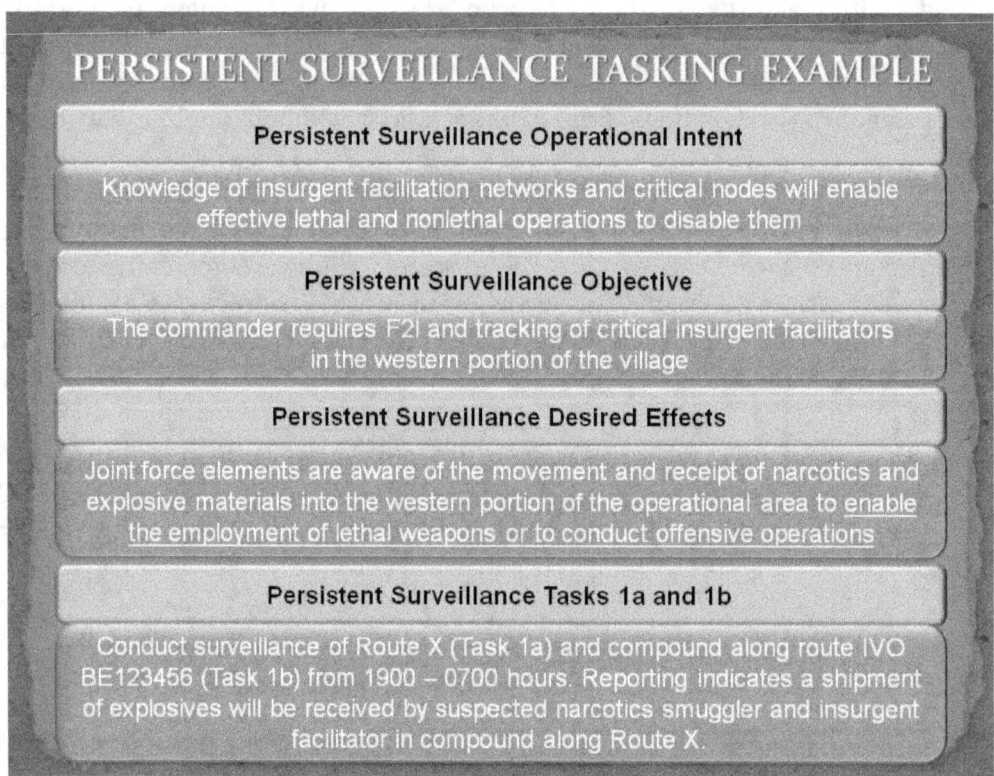

Figure VI-2. Persistent Surveillance Terminology

g.   A notional tasking example is illustrated in Figure VI-3.

PERSISTENT SURVEILLANCE TASKING EXAMPLE

Persistent Surveillance Operational Intent

Knowledge of insurgent facilitation networks and critical nodes will enable effective lethal and nonlethal operations to disable them

Persistent Surveillance Objective

The commander requires F2I and tracking of critical insurgent facilitators in the western portion of the village

Persistent Surveillance Desired Effects

Joint force elements are aware of the movement and receipt of narcotics and explosive materials into the western portion of the operational area to enable the employment of lethal weapons or to conduct offensive operations

Persistent Surveillance Tasks 1a and 1b

Conduct surveillance of Route X (Task 1a) and compound along route IVO BE123456 (Task 1b) from 1900 – 0700 hours. Reporting indicates a shipment of explosives will be received by suspected narcotics smuggler and insurgent facilitator in compound along Route X.

Figure VI-3. Persistent Surveillance Tasking Example

2. **Assessing Persistent Surveillance**

a. Assessing PS missions involves examining both quantitative and qualitative measures of performance and effectiveness, respectively. A PS operation assessment contains three distinct phases (Figure VI-4):

    (1) Phase I – PS Asset Performance

    (2) Phase II – PS Mission Performance

    (3) Phase III – PS Mission Effectiveness.

b. The goal is to conduct Phase I and II assessments as soon as the PS mission is completed. Phase III analysis should begin as soon as possible; however, it may take time for changes in the operating environment and/or adversary to be observed.

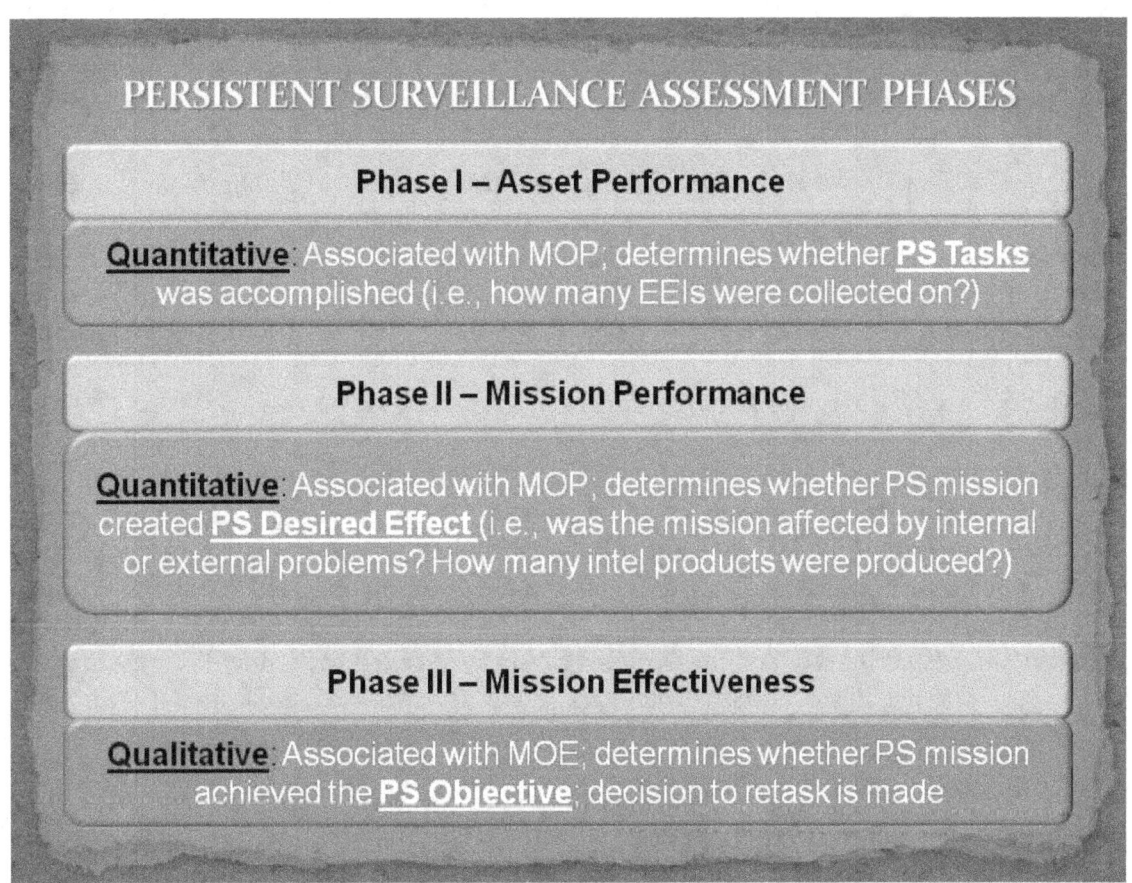

Figure VI-4. Persistent Surveillance Assessment Phases

c. Phases I and II are primarily a quantitative analysis of key metrics associated with PS operations MOPs. These phases are conducted with input from decision-makers, field units, collection managers, and PED personnel. Phase III is a qualitative analysis of MOEs focused on evaluating how well the collection operation met the PS Objective(s).

Both phases II and III provide data useful in determining re-tasking requirements. A procedure for collection of data and assessment through each of the phases follows in the sections below.

3. Measuring Performance

a. Phase I – Asset Performance

(1) Conducted within the first hour after a PS operation, Phase I assesses the PS Asset's activities in achieving the <u>PS Tasks</u> (definition above). This phase is exclusively quantitative in nature. Given the focus of Phase I, the MOP is focused on answering the PS Tasks associated with the PS mission. There are three metrics for Phase I:

(a) **Metric 1:** Number of EEIs tasked in the PS mission

(b) **Metric 2:** Number of EEIs collected during the PS mission

(c) **Metric 3:** The percent of PS mission EEIs collected against (EEIs Collected/EEIs Tasked) * 100 (This is also known as the percent complete (%C) of the PS mission).

(2) **For Phase I, the key metric is Metric 3, the %C.** High %C values are desirable. This metric gives the PS assessor the **first indication of the PS mission's success/failure in achieving the PS Objective**, whether it was F2I, target tracking, change detection, or a determination of the level or type of activity (pattern of life), or a combination of these objective types.

b. Phase II – Mission Performance

(1) Conducted within the first hour or as soon as possible after a PS mission, Phase II assesses the PS mission in achieving the <u>PS Desired Effect</u> (definition above). For the most part, Phase II is generally quantitative in nature; however, qualitative analysis in making re-tasking decisions or assessing internal/external problems affecting PS mission accomplishment is also appropriate. Given the focus of Phase II, the MOP is focused on answering if the PS Desired Effect associated with the PS mission was achieved. For the Phase II assessment, there are six specific PS Desired Effect MOP metrics:

(a) **Metric 1:** Number of intelligence products produced from PS data supporting the desired PS Desired Effect

(b) **Metric 2:** Number of deliberately planned and ad hoc/dynamic re-tasking events to support the PS mission:

<u>1</u>. FMV

2. Ground Moving Target Indicators (GMTI)

3. HUMINT

4. IMINT

5. MASINT

6. SIGINT

(c) **Metric 3:** Number of EEIs not collected due to:

1. Internal Problems (IPs)[7]

2. External Problems (EPs)[8]

(d) **Metric 4:** Percentage of Missions affected by Internal Problems (%IP): (Number of EEIs affected by IPs (EEIIP)/Number of EEIs Tasked) * 100

(e) **Metric 5:** Percentage of Missions affected by External Problems (%EP): (Number of EEIs affected by EP (EEIEP)/Number of EEIs Tasked) * 100

(f) **Metric 6: Percentage of Missions affected by Internal & External Problems (%EIP) =((EEIIP + EEIEP) /Tasked EEI) * 100**

(2) **For Phase II, the key metrics are Metric 1, 2, and 6.** Metric 1 provides the PS assessor an indication of the number of intelligence products being generated to support the PS mission, i.e., the potential return on investment of the PS mission. Metric 2 provides the PS assessor an indication of the number of collections tasked to multiple assets and the complexity of the PS mission. **Finally, Metric 6 provides the PS assessor a dash board indicator of the percentage of PS missions that have been affected due to both internal and external problems (%EIP) and therefore might need to be re-tasked.**

(3) Combined with the %C from Phase I, the %EIP is a key indicator that assists the assessor in making any potential recommendations for re-tasking the PS mission. For example, if during a high priority PS mission the %C was low and the %EIP was high, a PS assessor might make a recommendation to re-task the PS mission during Phase II. A Phase II recommendation for re-tasking is optional. A more complete re-tasking determination is recommended during Phase III, which combines both the Phase I and II quantitative MOP with the more qualitative Phase III MOE metrics. A good example of a Phase II recommendation to re-task would involve a very low %C and very high %EP due to weather. If the weather breaks within the timeframe of the PS mission, a recommendation to re-task the mission, based on Phase II results may be warranted.

4. Measuring Effectiveness

a. **Phase III – Mission Effectiveness**. Phase III assesses whether the PS mission achieves the PS objective (definition above).[9] The Phase III MOE is focused on answering if the PS mission achieved the PS objective and supported operations. Phase III also combines the Phase I and II quantitative MOE with the Phase III qualitative MOP to make a recommendation on the need to re-task the PS mission to support operational objectives. There are two Phase III PS Objective MOE metrics:

(1) **Metric 1**: Did the PS mission achieve the PS objective?

(2) **Metric 2**: Did the PS mission support the operational objectives?

b. The Phase III assessment focuses on asking the qualitative question concerning whether the PS mission succeeded in providing decision-makers and supported units with the answers to the original questions that triggered the operational need for the PS mission (PS Objective). Collaboration between intelligence and operations personnel is critical at this phase and all those involved should be given an opportunity to contribute to this phase of the assessment. For Phase III, the PS assessor should ask the two metric questions to decision-makers, operations managers, and field units as well as key collection and PED personnel.

c. Analysis of a PS mission may begin during the mission and may take several hours to complete, but should be conducted as soon as possible. **Every effort must be made to adhere to established assessment timelines within the unit in order to have as rapid an impact as possible on future collection opportunities**. Given the reality that it takes time for an effect to resonate throughout the operating environment and with the adversary, Phase III will take more time to complete than Phase I and II.

5. Re-tasking the Persistent Surveillance Mission

When the Phase III metrics are completed, an assessment is made of the need to re-task the PS mission. To make such a recommendation, the assessment must first take into consideration whether the PS Objective was met. This is best ascertained by answers to Phase III metric questions which are the result of the entire PS operational process.[10] Additionally, the recommendation to re-task must take into account the Phase I and II metric results. A close examination of the percent complete (Phase I), the number of intelligence products produced (Phase II), and the percentage of missions affected by external problems needs to be taken into consideration from an economy of force perspective. For example, low percent of completion and intelligence products produced, coupled with a high percentage of missions affected by external problems and a lower priority PS mission, might not warrant the further expenditure of collection assets to support the PS Objective.

6. Reporting the PS Mission Evaluation

The results of the assessment process are captured in a short three page PS Assessment Report. Broken out into three sections, the PS Assessment Report is matched precisely against the metrics for the three phases of the PS assessment process. Pages one and two follow the PS assessment process. Page three provides the assessor with a method to qualitatively assess, in a descriptive manner, the PS operation. Figures VI-5 and VI-6 below provide an example of a notional PS Assessment Report. A blank PS Assessment Report form is provided in Appendix C.

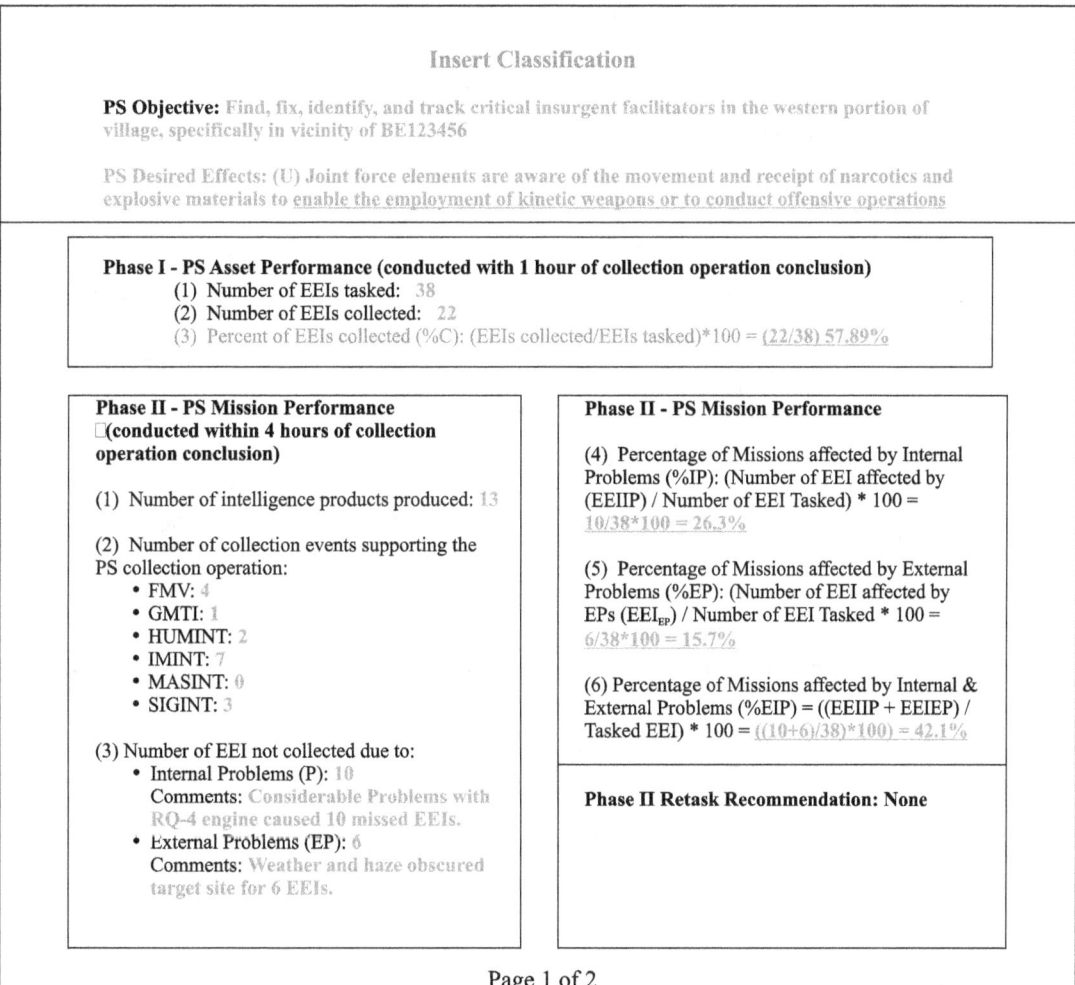

Figure VI-5. Example Persistent Surveillance Assessment Report, Phases I and II

Classification

PS Objective: Find, fix, identify, and track critical insurgent facilitators in the western portion of village, specifically in vicinity of BE123456

PS Desired Effects: (U) Joint force elements are aware of the movement and receipt of narcotics and explosive materials to <u>enable the employment of kinetic weapons or to conduct offensive operations</u>

Phase III - PS Mission Effectiveness

(1) Did the PS operation achieve the PS Objective? Yes, shipment was tracked and intercepted.

(2) Did the PS operation support the operation objectives of the echelon(s) it was supporting? Yes. Reported shipment of explosive materials was tracked and intercepted at the home of suspected insurgent facilitator in compound IVO BE123456. Insurgent facilitator and three others were detained and awaiting questioning.

Recommendation to Retask: PS Objective met. No need to retask.

PS Asset	PS Task Ia		PS Task Ib	
	Usage %	*Effectiveness*	*Usage %*	*Effectiveness*
SIGINT	100%	◉	0%	○
RQ-4	50%	○	100%	◉
HUMINT	30%	○	50%	◉

Effectiveness:
Not used: ○   Limited effectiveness: ◉   Effective: ○   Highly Effective: ◉

Page 2 of 2
Insert Classification

Figure VI-6. Example Persistent Surveillance Assessment Report, Phase III

CHAPTER VII
OPERATIONAL IMPLICATIONS

1. **General**

    a. In order to have effective and efficient persistent surveillance, the joint community needs to integrate persistent surveillance into existing doctrine and provide persistent surveillance training to commanders and staffs.

    b. The doctrine and training needs to highlight the necessity of an established and common method for tracking persistent surveillance requirements across the joint force; the need for a common operational picture to visualize the requirements as they relate to the operational environment, the joint force and adversary capabilities; and the assessment of collection operations required to capture the measures of effectiveness and measures of performance required to assess asset performance, mission performance, and mission effectiveness.

2. **Policy**

    a. The Department of Defense Capstone Concept for Joint Operations, with its institutional implications, seeks to create "greater adaptability and versatility across the force to cope with the uncertainty, complexity, unforeseeable change and persistent conflict that will characterize the future operating environment.

    b. Existing policy addresses the requirements for persistent surveillance as a part of existing collection missions.

    c. A signed Defense Collection Management Doctrine, Organization, Training, Materiel, Leadership and Education, Personnel, Facilities, and Policy (DOTMLPF-P) Change Recommendation, recommends codifying Department of Defense instructions on collection management by establishing authorities, responsibilities and standards in the Defense Collection Management Enterprise (DCME). The DCME must be capable of performing collection management activities across the range of military operations and in all strategic, operational, and tactical operating environments.

3. **Doctrine**

    a. Joint Doctrine does not address persistent surveillance as a distinct sub-function of collection management, but does mention its importance. Joint doctrine does not yet consistently define persistent surveillance using the agreed upon definition cited above.

    b. Updates to Joint Doctrine should address procedures and organizational changes for linking multi-disciplined ISR strategies and linking them to established operations planning, intelligence planning, and target planning. These strategies should also have linkage to ISR force management, ISR operations management, and ISR assessment.

c.   Updates to Joint Doctrine should clarify the requirements for conducting persistent surveillance operations, to include the responsibilities of Commander's and their staffs.   These requirements are consistent with current collection practices, explaining and expanding the responsibilities for specific ISR operations.

d.   Existing doctrine addressing persistent surveillance needs to highlight the importance of tracking, visualization and assessment as discussed in this handbook.

e.   Doctrine needs to codify the roles and responsibilities of commanders and staffs before, during, and after persistent surveillance missions.

f.   Doctrine concerning the planning and operations of collection missions must stress the complexity and resource intensive nature of these missions.

g.   The primary joint publications that likely need to add a more robust discussion of persistent surveillance include the following:

(1) JP 1-02, *DOD Dictionary of Military and Associated Terms.*

(2) JP 2-0, *Joint Intelligence.*

(3) JP 2-01, *Joint and National Intelligence Support to Military Operations.*

(4) JP 2-01.3, *Joint Intelligence Preparation of the Operational Environment.*

(5) JP 3-0, *Joint Operations.*

(6) JP 3-05.1, *Joint Special Operations Task Force Operations.*

(7) JP 3-07.4, *Joint Counterdrug Operations.*

(8) JP 3-26, *Counterterrorism.*

(9) JP 3-33, *Joint Task Force Headquarters.*

(10) JP 3-50, *Personnel Recovery.*

(11) JP 3-60, *Joint Targeting.*

(12) JP 5-0, *Joint Operation Planning.*

4.   Organization

Persistent surveillance planning, execution and assessment happen within existing planning, operations and intelligence activities.   There is no reason to create a separate persistent surveillance group that exists outside of such current organizations as the

JCMB, Targeting Board or Joint Intelligence and Operations Center. To create a different organization would be detrimental to the overall planning and operations functions of the joint force and the integration of persistent surveillance into existing joint operations.

5. Training

a. There is a need to establish a training program for operations and intelligence personnel that includes: prioritization of operational requirements based on CDR's intent, all-source collection requirements, ISR strategy development, and ISR planning, execution, and assessment. The scope of collection training includes skills for assessing the effectiveness of collection operations, collaboration with customers for satisfaction of collection requirements, and an evaluation and feedback process for adjusting ISR strategies, recommending collection priority changes, and reallocating ISR assets.

b. Persistent surveillance operation requirements need to be added to existing Operations, Planning, and Intelligence courseware, as well as included in leadership curriculum.

c. A review of Service and joint training indicates a need for synchronized training on the principles, requirements, and processes to conduct persistent surveillance.

d. Training on the tracking, visualization and assessment solutions developed to meet persistent surveillance should be developed, and included in existing targeting, collection management and ISR planning curriculum.

e. Training should also include integration of both traditional and non-traditional ISR capabilities and resources into all-source ISR plans and strategies.

6. Materiel

a. There are no materiel solutions envisioned for this process, but it is designed to effectively integrate a variety of materiel solutions (such as unmanned aircraft system [UAS] capability and visualization tools) in order to conduct persistent surveillance missions. To properly conduct persistent surveillance, a visualization tool that has visibility across all echelons and all services is required.

b. There also is no need for the services as part of a Joint force to develop or acquire new tools and applications for use during collection planning or ISR strategy modifications during ongoing collection operations.

7. Leadership and Education

a. Leader education within Joint Professional Military Education curricula should focus on understanding the processes, capabilities, and limitations of collection operations.

b.   The tracking of requirements, visualization of the entire environment (including all blue forces) and the proper continual assessment of the ongoing persistent surveillance operation require strong leadership that has been trained in the persistent surveillance process.

c.   Education for service leaders at all echelons that includes planning and conducting collection operations should include information on the specific requirements for decision makers during the planning, execution, and assessment of persistent surveillance missions.

d.   Senior leadership seminars conducted by the Service Components, and Command and Staff Colleges geared towards operational commanders, should include the issues and requirements of persistent surveillance within Joint Operations dealing with collection planning and operations.

8.   **Personnel**

a.   DIA has recommended that collection management become its own career field. If the Services agree, then this career field would be the most logical one to concentrate persistent surveillance training and doctrine on.

b.   Air Force and Army training centers have already begun discussions for specific career training relating to collection management.

c.   A collection management career field within the Service Components should not only address training and certification, but an assignment tracking system.

9.   **Facilities**

No solution is currently being considered that would expand or create DOD facilities.

10.   **Conclusion**

a.   The DCME must be capable of performing across the range of military operations and in all tactical, operational, and strategic environments.

b.   Information needs for commanders, planners, and requests for information from operations and intelligence personnel are transformed in collection requirements, ISR strategies, and collection tasks for "Mission Focused Operations."

c.   Requirements for persistent surveillance need to be included in current collection management doctrine and training.

APPENDIX A
PERSISTENT SURVEILLANCE
RECOMMENDED ACTIVITIES FOR PLANNERS

1. **Coordinate across Echelons and Functions**

Coordinate closely with the collection management team, Joint ISR Manager (JISRM), decision-makers, and others (as required) to apply principles of improved visualization, tracking and assessment of persistent surveillance missions.

2. **Use the Collection Asset Baseline**

Populate and maintain the CAB spreadsheet to provide a consolidated place for all ISR asset TCPED requirements.

3. **Feed the Common Operating Picture**

Coordinate with the collection management team, joint ISR manager, Global Command and Control System (GCCS) operators, and others feeding the COP/UDOP to ensure the following relevant data is associated with each asset track to the maximum extent possible:

a. Asset name

b. Asset call sign

c. Sensor type(s)

d. Subordination

e. Current mission

f. Specific NAIs being collected

g. Priority of tasking

h. Units supporting

i. Launch/on-station/off-station/recovery times

j. Hyperlink to data feed from sensor (if available)

k. Dynamic re-task information (chat room, POC email, phone number, etc.) or coordination circuit.

4. **Consolidate Requirements and Disseminate**

Consolidate collection requirements on appropriate network and create a consolidated collection requirements matrix (CCRM) and sanitize CCRM for posting and further dissemination on US and coalition networks.

5. **Conduct Assessment of Persistent Surveillance Missions**

Coordinate with required personnel to conduct Phase I, II, and III assessment processes and coordinate dynamic re-task recommendation stemming from those processes with collection management team, joint ISR manager, and unit tasking authorities as required.

APPENDIX B
BASELINE COLLECTION ASSET OPERATIONAL VIEW

1. Overview and Description

a. **Background**. Employment of JIPS principles concerning visualization, tracking and assessment of collection operations requires all echelons to develop a comprehensive, common and readily adaptable view of the collection capabilities in a theater of operations. During the JIPS experimentation efforts it was determined that a baseline set of information for each national-to-tactical collection asset in a given theater was needed to enable improved persistent surveillance operations. The Baseline Collection Asset Operational View (BCAOV) was created to provide this capability. It is designed to be a comprehensive display of all relevant information on national, theater and below collection assets and complete TCPED requirements. The BCAOV would be accessible to all echelons and can be readily tailored and updated based on the needs of each user.

b. **Method**. While an automated, searchable, web-accessible database would ultimately provide the greatest utility, the decision was made to develop and maintain the BCAOV data in a Microsoft Excel spreadsheet, given the ease with which data could be shared and viewed in that format. The first step that must be done in creating a BCAOV is research to determine how to leverage ISR assets in order to answer the Commander's Priority Intelligence Requirements (PIRs), which is the same type of research a deploying collection management staff would need to conduct prior to entering their theater of operations. Figure B-1 depicts the methodology that a Collection Manager would employ in this step and the critical questions that must be answered in order to rapidly satisfy the PIRs. Once these questions are answered, the information is used to populate the BCAOV spreadsheet. This format allows for compatibility and simple dissemination throughout the theater and can be easily amended for specific unit needs. It provides a standardized framework for gathering and organizing data about collection assets and their associated tasking and PED processes that can inform the development of more advanced tools for cataloging and organizing this data for each theater of operations.

c. **Purpose**. The primary purpose of the BCAOV tool is to provide users at all echelons in the theater of operations with the baseline data that could be used to more rapidly plan deliberate collection missions, to aid in understanding how to re-task an asset for near-term or immediate collection requirements, and to provide information on PED capabilities that would support assessment of collection activities.

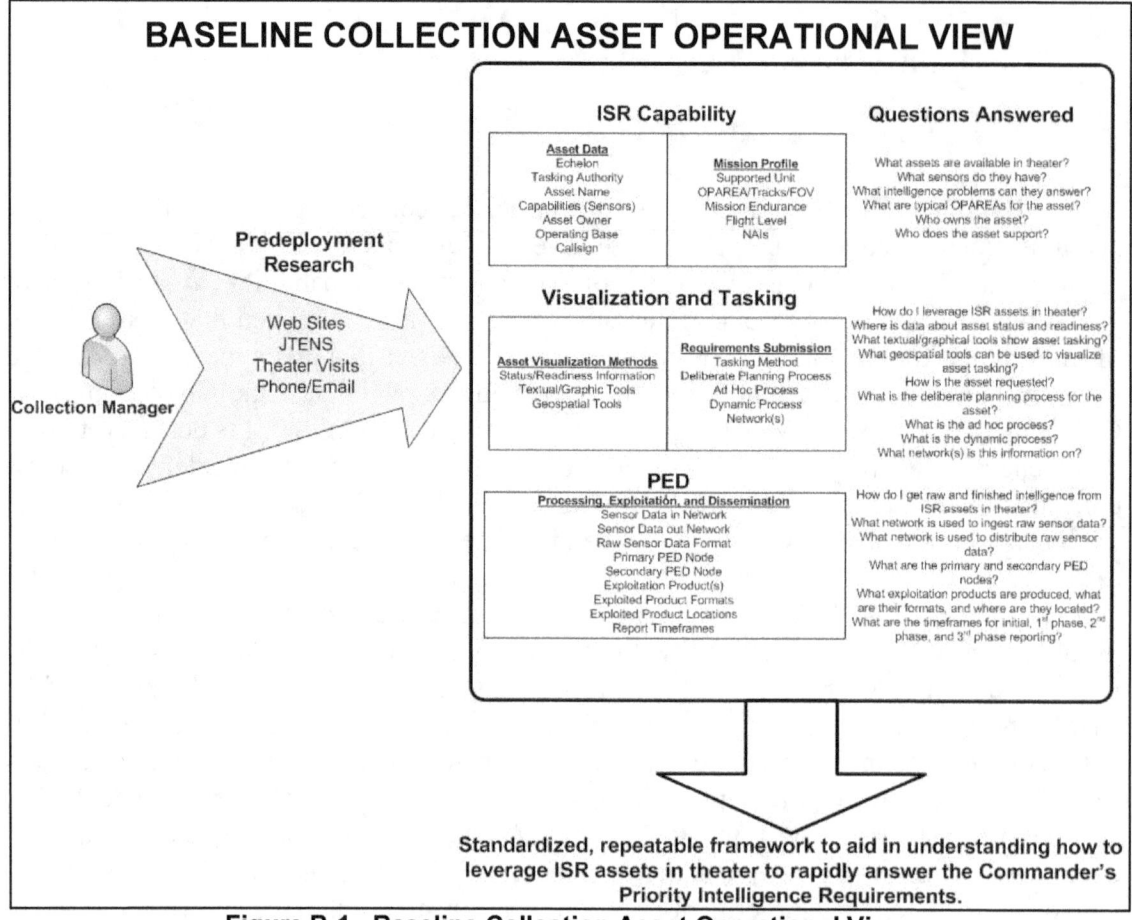

Figure B-1. Baseline Collection Asset Operational View

2. BCAOV Spreadsheet Categories and Fields

a. **Asset Data**

(1) Echelon with tasking authority over the asset

(2) Specific unit/command with tasking authority

(3) Asset name

(4) Sensor types/intelligence capabilities

(5) Asset owner

(6) Operating base

(7) Call sign

(8) Unit(s)/Missions the asset is supporting

b. **Mission Profile**

    (1) Typical Operational area, track, or orbits used or asset geo-location

    (2) Endurance

    (3) Flight level/altitude

    (4) Specific NAI or target area of interest

c. **Tasking Methods**

    (1) Deliberate Planning

        (a) Process (Who does the request go to? What is the format of the request? What system is used?)

        (b) Communication paths and specific addressees (Message, email, chat, etc.)

        (c) Timelines from asset request to collection

    (2) Ad hoc tasking (Ad hoc requests are those submitted prior to Air Tasking Order execution, typically a collection request that requires action in less than 24 hours.)

        (a) Process (Who does the request go to? What is the format of the request? What system is used?)

        (b) Communication paths and specific addressees (Message, email, chat, etc.)

        (c) Timelines from asset request to collection

    (3) Dynamic re-tasking (Dynamic requests are those requiring immediate servicing and are typically requested via chat or voice using an 8-line format that defines: Desired ISR Support or Effect; Target Name; Target Location; Essential Elements of Information; Latest Time Information of Value; Reporting instruction, i.e. circuit, format, point of contact; ISR asset detection concerns; and Area for de-confliction.)

        (a) Process (Who does the request go to? What is the format of the request? What system is used?)

        (b) Communication paths and specific addressees (Message, email, chat, etc.)

        (c) Timelines from asset request to collection

d. **Asset Visualization Methods**

(1) Asset status/readiness information

(2) Textual/graphical aids (collection plan, planned intelligence day {PID} graphic, etc.

(3) Geospatial tools (Global Command and Control System {GCCS}, Command Post of the Future [CPOF], Google Earth, etc.)

e. **Requirements (visualization and tracking)**

(1) Method(s) (spreadsheet, ISR Synchronization Tool [IST], Planning Tool for Resource Integration, Synchronization and Management [PRISM], etc.)

(2) Network(s)

f. **Processing, Exploitation and Dissemination (PED)**

(1) Method/System (web posting, e-mail, chat, ROVER, etc.)

(2) Format (text, JPEG image, XML file, h.264, etc.)

(3) Network

(4) Timeframe (direct download of sensor data, quick-look report, 1st, 2nd, and 3rd phase exploitation report, etc.)

3. **BCAOV Sample Spreadsheet Entries**

Parts 1 through 3 of Table B-1 below provide examples of a completed baseline asset collection operational view. Below is a list of the specific data fields that need to be populated within the BCAOV (with sample entries in italics) in order for it to serve as a useful tool in planning persistent surveillance operations.

a. **Asset Data**

(1) Echelon: *Brigade (BDE)*

(2) Tasking Authority: *Task Force (TF) Normandy*

(3) Asset: *Predator*

(4) Capabilities: *EO/IR/FMV*

(5) Asset Owner: *18 RS*

(6) Operating Base: *Fort Huachuca (FHU)*

(7) Call sign: *COPPER*

b. **Mission Profile**

(1) Supporting (which unit): *TF Normandy*

(2) OPAREA/Tracks/FOV: *CEN PT: 123456.01N 0123456.70W*

(3) Mission Endurance: *6 Hours*

(4) Flight Level: *100*

(5) NAIs: *As identified*

c. **Tasking Methods**

(1) Deliberate Planning Process: *Requirements submitted via the chain of command using ISR Support Tool (IST), e-mail, chat, or voice and consolidated in Component Prioritized Collection List (CPCL). Requirements prioritized and tasked via the JCMB. (Fragmentary Order/Collection Emphasis Message)*

(2) Deliberate Planning Network: *Coalition and US*

(3) Deliberate Planning Timeline: *>24 hours*

(4) Ad Hoc/Dynamic Process: *Requirements submitted via the chain of command using TF Edge chat room or voice over internet protocol (VOIP) to the Senior Intelligence Duty Officer (SIDO) in 8 line format. SIDO coordinates with required personnel to validate and action the requirement.*

(5) Ad Hoc/Dynamic Process Network: *Coalition*

(6) Ad Hoc/Dynamic Process Timeline: *Ad hoc = <24 hours & prior to air tasking order (ATO) execution, Dynamic = immediate*

d. **Asset Visualization Methods**

(1) Status/Readiness: *Asset Status posted to wiki page and Combined Air Operations Center (CAOC) portal*

(2) Textual/Graphic: *Daily Collection Plan (on Coalition and US networks), Air Tasking Order (ATO) Collection Emphasis Message (CEM) Annex*

(3) Geospatial: *Current employment: GCCS I3, Google Earth Common Operational Picture (COP) feed, IST; Historical and Future: IST*

e. **Requirements**

(1) Tracking Method: *IST, Consolidated Collection Requirements Matrix (CCRM)*

(2) Network: *Coalition and US*

f. **PED**

(1) Sensor Data-In Network: *Coalition*

(2) Sensor Data-Out Network: *Coalition and US*

(3) Raw Sensor Data Format: *H.264, MPEG-4*

(4) Primary PED Node: *DCGS-A*

(5) Secondary PED Node: *DCGS-SOF*

(6) Exploitation Product(s): *Enters on Coalition network via GCS or ROVER. Exposed on Coalition network via National Geospatial Agency (NGA) Visualization Services (NVS) and also disseminated to DCGS on US network via guard and multi-caster.*

(7) Exploited Product Format(s): *MPEG-4, Others?*

(8) Exploited Product Location(s): *NVS, DCGS Federation*

(9) Network(s): *Coalition*

(10) Initial Report Timeframe: *Chat – Immediate*

(11) 1st Phase Report Timeframe: *24 hours*

(12) 2nd Phase Report Timeframe: *48-72 hours*

(13) 3rd Phase Report Timeframe: *72+ hours*

4. **BCAOV Complete Spreadsheet Examples**

The intention is for all ISR planners, collection managers, analysts, operators and decision makers to have a full view of all assets in theater and at the national level supporting that theater. The following tables display the components of the BCAOV. **When using the spreadsheet in Microsoft Excel, connect all components in a row for a full operational view**.

Asset Data						Mission Profile					
Echelon	Tasking Authority	Asset	Capabilities	Asset Owner	Operating Base	Callsign	Supporting	OPAREA/Tracks/FOV	Mission Endurance	Flight Level	NAIs
National	*ISAF JC*	*vOP/IR*	*IR*	-	-	-	*Various*	-	-	-	*N/A*
JTF/RC	ISAF JC, RC-SW-Forward, RC-SW Rear	U-2S ASARS-2	SAR/GMTI/RAS-1R	9RW	BAB	PINON	TF Normandy	UW PT1: 1104119W / 312654N; U2 PT2: 1095513W / 312741N; U2 PT3: 1095556W / 314125N; U2 PT4: 1104314W / 314018N	4 hours	640	TANGO, ARROW, LMA
JTF/RC	ISAF JC, RC-SW-Forward, RC-SW Rear	EP-3E	EO/IR/SIGINT	VQ-1	NTD	DEEPSEA	TF Rock Steady	EP-3 A: 1104434.88W / 313809.24N; EP-3 B: 1101606.35W / 313504.97N; EP-3 C: 1094449.60W / 313431.03N	5 hours	260	N/A
BDE	TF Normandy	Predator	EO/IR/FMV	9RW	FHU	FIREBIRD	TF Normandy	CEN PT: 1101026.90W / 312914.01N	6 hours	100	STONE
BN	TF Rock Steady	BETSS-C RAID Tower	EO/IR/FMV	1st BN	FHU	BOOMER	TF Rock Steady	CEN PT: 1151646.70W / 314532.01N	24 hours	N/A	TOMCAT

Table B-1. Baseline Collection Asset Operational View, Part 1

Asset		Asset Visualization Methods		Requirements	
	Status/ Readiness	Textual/Graphic	Geospa ial	Tasking Method	Network
vOPIR	NRO Site - JWICS	Daily Collection Plan (SIPRNET)	PRISM - JWICS	PRISM, CCRM	SIPRNET
U-2S ASARS-2	CAOC Portal	Daily Collection Plan (SIPRNET), RSTA Annex	GCCS I3 (Current); Google Ear h COP (Current); IST (historical, current, planned)	PRISM, CCRM	SIPRNET
EP-3E (HITS4.0) #1	Theater Collec ions Portal	Daily Collection Plan (AMN, SIPRNET), RSTA Annex	GCCS I3 (Current); Google Ear h COP (Current); IST (historical, current, planned)	PRISM, CCRM	AMN, SIPRNET
Predator	CAOC Portal	Daily Collection Plan (AMN, SIPRNET), CEM	GCCS I3 (Current); Google Ear h COP (Current); IST (historical, current, planned)	PRISM, CCRM	AMN, SIPRNET
BETSS-C RAID	Asset Status Wiki	Daily Collection Plan (AMN, SIPRNET), CEM	IST (historical, current, planned)	IST, CCRM	AMN, SIPRNET

Table B-1. Baseline Collection Asset Operational View, Part 2

Asset		PED										
	Network	Sensor Data in Network	Sensor Data out Network	Raw Sensor Data Format	Primary PED Node	Secondary PED Node	Exploitation Product(s)	Exploited Product Format(s)	Exploited Product Location(s)	Network(s)	Report Timeframes (initial, 1st phase, 2nd phase, 3rd phase)
vOPIR	SIPRNET	JWICS	SIPRNET	NITF	DGS-1	DGS-3	IPIR, GEOINT Products	Text, JPG, NITF, Office Product	Imagery Product Library (IPL), WARP	SIPRNET	Initial - 6 hours, 1st phase - 24 hours, 2nd phase - 72 hours, 3rd phase - 7-21 days
U-2S ASARS-2	AMN, SIPRNET	AF DCGSWAN	SIPRNET	SAR NITF 2.1	DGS-1	DGS-5	Finished intel products sent via guard to DCGS DIB and coalition partners.	Text, JPG, MS Office Product, Other	IPL, Other places?	SIPRNET, AMN	Initial - 4 hours, 1st phase -12 hours, 2nd phase - 24-48 hours, 3rd phase - 7-14 days
EP-3E (HITS4.0) #1	AMN, SIPRNET	SIPRNET	SIPRNET Tear line AMN	N/A	Onboard aircraft	N/A	Chat, Voice, Spot Report, Post-missi-on report	Text		SIPRNET, AMN	
Predator	AMN, SIPRNET	SIPRNET	SIPRNET	MPEG-2	DCGS--A	DGS-1	Full Motion Video (FMV) stream, Annotated imagery	MPEG-2, H.264, JPG clips, PowePoint	IPL, NVS, Coalition Data Broker (CDB)	SIPRNET, AMN	Initial - chat immediate, 1st phase -8 hours, 2nd phase - 24 hours, 3rd phase - 72 hours
BETSS-C RAID	AMN, SIPRNET	AMN	AMN	H.264	DCGS--A MB	TMAAS	FMV, Still Clips	H.264, MPEG-2, JPG Clips	NVS, DCGS Federation.	SIPRNET, AMN	Initial - chat immediate, 1st phase -12 hours, 2nd and 3rd phase - N/A
KEY											
Unknown Data											
Unconfirmed Data											

Table B-1. Baseline Collection Asset Operational View, Part 3

Intentionally Blank

APPENDIX C
PERSISTENT SURVEILLANCE ASSESSMENT REPORT FORM

PS Objective:

Operational Objective:

Phase I - PS Asset Performance (conducted with 1 hour of collection operation conclusion)
  (4) Number of EEIs tasked: ____
  (5) Number of EEIs collected: ____
  (6) Percent of EEIs collected (%C): (EEIs collected/EEIs tasked)*100 = _____

Phase II - PS Mission Performance (conducted within 4 hours of collection operation conclusion)

(3) Number of intelligence products produced: ___

(4) Number of collection events supporting the PS collection operation:
  • FMV: ____
  • GMTI: ____
  • HUMINT: ____
  • IMINT: ____
  • MASINT: ____
  • SIGINT: ____

(3) Number of EEI not collected due to:
  • Internal Problems (IP): ____
    Comments:
  • External Problems (EP): ____
    Comments:

Phase II - PS Mission Performance

(4) Percentage of Missions affected by Internal Problems (%IP): (Number of EEI affected by (EEIIP) / Number of EEI Tasked) * 100 = ____

(5) Percentage of Missions affected by External Problems (%EP): (Number of EEI affected by EPs (EEI$_{EP}$) / Number of EEI Tasked * 100 = ____

(6) Percentage of Missions affected by Internal & External Problems (%EIP) = ((EEIIP + EEIEP) / Tasked EEI) * 100 =

Phase II Retask Recommendation:

Page 1 of 2

Figure C-1. Persistent Surveillance Assessment Report Form, Phases I and II

Classification

PS Objective:

Operational Objective:

Phase III - PS Mission Effectiveness

    (3) Did the PS operation achieve the PS Objective?

    (4) Did the PS operation support the operation objectives of the echelon(s) it was supporting?

Recommendation to Retask:

PS Asset	PS Task 1		PS Task 2	
	Usage %	*Effectiveness*	*Usage %*	*Effectiveness*

Effectiveness:
Not used: ○   Limited effectiveness: ◉   Effective: ○   Highly Effective: ◉

Page 2 of 2
Insert Classification

Figure C-2. Persistent Surveillance Assessment Report Form, Phase III

APPENDIX D
EXISTING POLICY AND GUIDANCE

1. Introduction

a. This appendix highlights a portion of existing policy and guidance throughout the Department of Defense on Persistent Surveillance. A large volume of work has been done on the topic of Persistent ISR by DOD and the services; this work served to inform the JIPS project and limit redundant research and experimentation.

b. Reviews of National-level, Department of Defense, Joint, and Service publications were conducted to understand where persistent surveillance fits in the scope of current doctrine, and what guidance, direction and lessons learned exists on the topic of persistent surveillance. The documentation below provides general summaries and/or key, relevant pieces of information that illuminate persistent surveillance capabilities and problems and have helped inform the JIPS project.

2. Department of Defense Level Guidance

a. *2006 Quadrennial Defense Review*, February 2006; "Intelligence, Surveillance, Reconnaissance (ISR)," pages 55-58:

(1) The ability of the future force to establish an "unblinking eye" over the battle-space through persistent surveillance will be key to conducting effective joint operations.

(2) The Department will increase investment in unmanned aerial vehicles to provide more flexible capabilities and will implement a new imagery intelligence approach focused on achieving persistent collection capabilities in cooperation with the Director of National Intelligence. Investments in moving target indicator and synthetic aperture radar capabilities, including Space Radar, will grow to provide a highly persistent capability to identify and track moving ground targets in denied areas.

b. *2010 Quadrennial Defense Review*, February 2010; "Succeed in Counterinsurgency, Stability and Counterterrorism Operations," page 22

The Department will expand manned and UASs for ISR. Long-dwell UASs, such as the Predator, Reaper, and other systems, have proven to be invaluable for monitoring activities in contested areas, enhancing situational awareness, protecting our forces, and assisting in targeting enemy fighters.

c. *Persistent Intelligence, Surveillance, and Reconnaissance: Planning and Direction Joint Integrating Concept, Version 1.0*, March 2007

(1) The central idea described in this Joint Integrating Concept is that persistence against an elusive target can be increased through the integrated,

synchronized management of ISR planning and direction. The need for persistence implies a need to detect, identify and characterize change in the structure, status and behavior of an elusive target. The integrated, synchronized management of planning and direction is achieved through five enabling capabilities: integrated prioritization, multi-level tasking, global visibility, automated interfaces, and capable collection managers.

(2) More specifically:

(a) Integrated Planning and Prioritization -- Establish a multi-level priority system allowing collection assets at different echelons to understand how to respond to collection requests.

(b) Multi-level Tasking -- Enable taskings to flow down echelon as readily as they flow up-echelon to allow any asset with relevant capacity to satisfy the collection requirement.

(c) Global Visibility -- Provide virtual visibility, via automated toolsets, into the tasking, status, and capabilities of all ISR assets to those responsible for their real-time management and near-term planning.

(d) Automated Interfaces -- Enable rapid machine-to-machine interactions that provide multi-intelligence, multi-asset data on high priority intelligence problems.

(e) Training and Education -- Provide operators, intelligence analysts, and collection managers with a greater understanding of the capabilities of all ISR systems and how they can be applied to various intelligence problems.

(3) It is important to note that this Joint Integrating Concept does not advocate centralized management or changes in asset ownership. The situational awareness that results from global visibility allows expert collection managers to influence the ISR Enterprise to the benefit of the JFC. Moreover, integrated prioritization, multi-level tasking, and automated interfaces create a flexible enterprise that can rapidly concentrate an optimal mix of ISR assets in order to gain persistence.

d. *Capstone Concept for Joint Operations, Version 3.0*, January 2009:

(1) Improvements in irregular warfare knowledge and capabilities are called for. Persistent surveillance is a critical enabler for irregular warfare.

(2) This document calls for an improvement in the ability to operate in an urban environment. For example, security operations in urban environments are complicated by a myriad of social, economic, religious, and other patterns. That presents challenges for persistent surveillance as well as opportunities to achieve success in this type of terrain.

3. **Defense Intelligence Operations Coordination Center Organization, Mission, and Operations**

   a. **Organization and Mission**. The Defense Intelligence Operations Coordination Center (DIOCC) provides a single organization to synchronize defense intelligence operations in support of combatant commands, and DOD and intelligence community (IC) requirements. DIOCC also improves the coordination and information sharing within DOD and the national IC. Additionally, DIOCC is instrumental in maximizing the effectiveness of DOD and national intelligence capabilities. On 1 October 2007, the SecDef directed the establishment of the DIOCC, merging the Defense Joint Intelligence Coordination Center, Joint Functional Component Command for Intelligence, Surveillance, and Reconnaissance (JFCC-ISR), and formed a support relationship as an interagency partner with the National Intelligence Coordination Center.

   b. **Operations**. DIOCC coordinates and integrates critical interaction among Defense mission partners with intelligence operations capabilities, and between those partners, the CCMDs, the National Intelligence Coordination Center, and other appropriate Office of the Director of National Intelligence elements. It enables prioritized and timely collaboration, interaction, and synchronization among mission partners to deliver intelligence capabilities whenever and wherever needed. The DIOCC provides enterprise management that is objective and transparent, facilitates all-source approaches, and enables intelligence sharing and a common global intelligence operations picture.

4. **Joint Doctrine**

   a. Joint doctrine has incorporated the concept of persistent surveillance into multiple publications. The JIPS project may pave the way forward for joint persistent ISR and collection management doctrine development in the future.

   b. JP 2-0, *Joint Intelligence*, June 2007. Persistent surveillance and dynamic ISR collection management are important throughout the execution of joint operations. An ISR strategy that fully integrates and optimizes the use of all available U.S., coalition, and host-nation ISR assets is essential to persistent surveillance.

   c. JP 2-01, *Joint and National Intelligence Support to Military Operations*, October 2004. The intelligence process is the basis for developing a collection strategy. A collection strategy is a systematic scheme to optimize the effective and efficient tasking of all capable, available, and appropriate collection assets and/or resources against requirements. Persistent surveillance is facilitated by the effective integration and synchronization of all theater and national ISR assets and resources in a coherent collection strategy.

5. Army Guidance

a. Department of the Army FMI 2-01 (FM 34-2), *Intelligence, Surveillance and Reconnaissance Synchronization*, November 2008. The goal of the Army conceptual discussion of joint persistent surveillance is to provide the right intelligence to the right person at the right time and in the right format focused to their requirements. The latest Army intelligence concepts are based on the fundamental Army ISR construct and recognize ISR as a combined arms mission. However, these concepts focus on balancing future requirements for providing or accessing combat information and intelligence in a networked environment to support ongoing operations while also supporting long-term intelligence analysis and planning and other staff functions.

b. Most of the concepts (and the "Tactical Persistent Surveillance" white paper) focus on the following:

(1) Embedded ISR synchronization capabilities.

(2) Improved ISR sensor capabilities and effective evaluation of ISR resources.

(3) Assured network communications capability.

(4) An enterprise approach to analysis, processing, and data or information access across units or organizations and echelons.

(5) Enhanced automated analytical tools to include planning and control, and analytical change detection capabilities.

6. Air Force Guidance

KEY TERM: GLOBAL VIGILANCE

The Air Force concept of Global Vigilance is the persistent capability to sense any entity on or below the surface, in air, space, and cyberspace to acquire information required to meet national security and national defense objectives.

a. **Headquarters Air Force ISR Agency**. *Intelligence, Surveillance, and Reconnaissance (ISR) CONOPS Draft*, March 2008:

(1) National and military decision makers depend on ISR for global vigilance and to understand the complex and uncertain environment in which they operate, allowing them to make rapid and reliable decisions.

(2) **Planning and Direction**. ISR planning is the ability to synchronize and integrate the activities of collection, processing, analysis, and dissemination resources to meet information requirements of military and civilian decision-makers. Since information demands will always exceed ISR supply, ISR planners must prioritize

information requirements against guidance and objectives. The four focus areas for transforming planning and direction include effects-based allocation, optimized sensor planning, comprehensive sensor tasking, and effective evaluation and feedback.

(3) **ISR Collection Capabilities – Dynamic Re-Tasking and Cross-Cueing**. To optimize ongoing collection against the evolving battlespace environment, ISR personnel must be able to visualize the entire battlespace to recommend collection reallocation and to synchronize operations to eliminate redundancy and increase effectiveness (interdependence). Key to this will be the ability to have access to and understand joint, civilian, and coalition activities. In order to achieve cross-domain dominance, we will need the ability to cross-cue from any sensor to any sensor across all domains. Further effectiveness will come from taking advantage of sensor netting from organic (HUMINT) and inorganic assets.

b. **Headquarters Air Force**. Air Force Doctrinal Document 2-9, *Intelligence, Surveillance, and Reconnaissance Operations*:

(1) The **Air Force perspective of surveillance** is that surveillance operations are sustained operations designed to gather information by a collector, or series of collectors, having timely response and persistent observation capabilities, a long dwell time and clear continuous collection capability.

(2) **Persistent and Global Reach**. Commanders require the ability to achieve on-demand reconnaissance and persistent surveillance throughout the operational environment. Modern collection requirements are increasingly focused on fleeting dispersed targets that present a markedly different signature from industrial-age targets such as large military formations and complex industrial facilities. To deny enemy sanctuaries of movement, Air Force ISR capabilities focus detailed collection against broad target areas for long periods of time, either through long-dwell sensors or a combination of more numerous short-dwell collectors. The combination of persistence and reach complicates enemy planning and reduces enemy choices while creating options for commanders.

(3) Changing situations may require that ISR assets be dynamically re-tasked from their preplanned mission to support new mission requirements. The capabilities of the asset being re-tasked will determine the success of the reassigned mission. For example, ISR assets with long loiter times or frequent revisit rates generally have the flexibility to respond to dynamic re-tasking.

Intentionally Blank

APPENDIX E
LESSONS LEARNED

1. Government Accountability Office (GAO) Report on Unmanned Aircraft Systems

The GAO Report titled "Unmanned Aircraft Systems: Advance Coordination and Increased Visibility Needed to Optimize Capabilities (GAO 07-836), published in July 2007, reported the following primary findings.

a. DOD components have developed guidance to facilitate the integration of UAS into combat operations; however, further steps are needed to coordinate the deployment of these assets. For example, DOD developed guidance for the tactical employment of UAS and a Joint UAS concept of Operations. This guidance is an important first step but does not address coordinating UAS and other ISR assets prior to deploying them to ongoing operations, which U.S. Central Command recognized is a critical factor in integrating UAS into combat operations. Until DOD addresses the need for DOD-wide advance coordination, it may continue to face challenges in successfully integrating UAS and other ISR assets into combat operations and may exacerbate integration challenges such as limited bandwidth.

b. DOD's approach to allocating and tasking its ISR assets, including UAS, hinders its ability to optimize the use of these assets because it does not consider the capabilities of all available ISR assets. The command charged with recommending how theater-level DOD ISR assets should be allocated to support operational requirements does not have awareness of all available ISR assets because DOD does not have a mechanism for obtaining this information. Similarly, the commander responsible for coordinating ongoing joint air operations does not have information on how assets controlled by tactical units are being used or what missions they've been tasked to support. Nor do tactical units have information on how theater-level assets and ISR assets embedded in other units are being tasked, which results in problems such as duplicative taskings. This lack of visibility occurs because DOD does not have a mechanism for tracking the missions both theater- and tactical-level ISR assets are supporting or how they are being used. Without an approach to allocation and tasking that includes a mechanism for considering all ISR capabilities, DOD may be unable to fully leverage all available ISR assets and optimize their use.

c. DOD is unable to fully evaluate the performance of its ISR assets because it lacks a complete set of metrics and does not consistently receive feedback to ensure the warfighter's needs were met. Although the joint functional component command for ISR has been tasked with developing ISR metrics, DOD currently assesses its ISR missions with limited quantitative metrics such as the number of targets planned versus captured. While these metrics are a good start, DOD officials acknowledge that the current metrics do not capture all of the qualitative considerations associated with measuring ISR asset effectiveness such as the cumulative knowledge provided by numerous ISR missions. There is an ongoing effort within DOD to develop additional quantitative as well as qualitative ISR metrics, but no DOD-wide milestones have been established. Furthermore, DOD guidance calls for an evaluation of the results of joint operations; however, DOD officials acknowledge that this feedback is not consistently occurring due to the fast pace of operations in theater. Without metrics and feedback, DOD may not be able to validate how well the warfighter's needs are being met, whether it is optimizing the use of existing assets, or which new systems would best support warfighting needs.

2. Joint Chiefs of Staff Persistent Intelligence, Surveillance, and Reconnaissance Joint Capabilities Document

a. The Joint Chiefs of Staff Persistent ISR Joint Capabilities Document (JCD), published in November 2007, reported the findings of the capabilities based assessment conducted for the Persistent ISR Joint Integrating Concept. Its top-level conclusions are discussed below.

(1) The JCD found only partial support for the Joint Integrating Concept hypothesis that improvements to ISR planning and direction will provide the JFC with more effective ISR support and increased persistence, "particularly against elusive, low-profile targets of interest" across the range of military operations. The potential for better planning and direction to improve ISR persistence is real and significant in some areas, but not against the area of greatest concern — elusive and low-profile targets.

(2) Elusive targets often require long periods of continuous-dwell collection. Furthermore, when elusive targets also present a low profile, this continuous-dwell collection is typically satisfied by sensors with narrow field of regard (FOR). Together, these characteristics do not present a significant opportunity for better planning and direction to improve persistence. Instead, for this subset of the ISR problem, it appears that large capacity shortfalls exist and must be overcome before planning and direction improvements alone will have a substantive impact on persistence.

(3) In situations where there is more overlap between sensors FOR, or where the need for continuous dwell is less and time-constraints are more flexible, there is significant opportunity for improvement through better planning and direction. In these circumstances, which can also be mitigated through greater collection capacity, resolving critical planning and direction capability gaps will result in persistence gains. The list of prioritized gaps and the following recommendations address this opportunity.

b. **Recommendations**. Based upon the capability gap prioritization, and in light of the findings above, this JCD recommends the following actions:

(1) Advocate for multi-intelligence collection strategies and implementation of related DOTMLPF initiatives, both ongoing and proposed.

(2) The capabilities based assessment finds that global visibility is a necessary pre-cursor to most, if not all, planning and direction improvements. Continued advancements in multi-intelligence, multi-platform collection initiatives, as well as

possible improvement efforts in integrated planning and prioritization and multi-level tasking, are dependent on dramatically improved global visibility.

    c.   **Gaps in Persistent ISR Capabilities**. The JCD cites eighteen gaps in persistent ISR capabilities. (Note: Nearly all of these were corroborated in other documents reviewed for the Baseline Assessment.) The first five are considered "Tier 1, Highest Priority." In descending priority order:

    (1) Inability to develop and implement multi-intelligence collection strategies.

    (2) Inability to leverage multi-asset, cooperative collection potential.

    (3) Inability to gain visibility into all collection requirements and pending collection tasks relevant to an information requirement and/or collection.

    (4) Inability to gain visibility and access to all data and products relevant to an information requirement and/or collection mission.

    (5) Inability to maintain requirement traceability (transparency and visibility) through the requirements process and the intelligence cycle.

    (6) Inability to detect and differentiate between intentionally and unintentionally redundant requirements and tasking.

    (7) Inability to dynamically re-task sensors, understand collection implications, and dynamically re-optimize collection plans.

    (8) Inability to maintain visibility on operational status of collection and PED assets.

    (9) Inability to prioritize and value (weight) collection requirements across intelligence disciplines, operating echelons and theaters.

    (10) Inability to re-allocate PED resources dynamically, understand implications and reoptimize.

    (11) Inability to integrate non-traditional, commercial, coalition, and civil ISR into the ISR enterprise.

    (12) Inability to measure contribution and impact of collections and products on the operational objective and associated RFI.

    (13) Inability to track discipline-specific task interdependencies, from within a multi-intelligence collection strategy, throughout the intelligence process.

(14) Inability to forecast probability of collection, for organic and non-organic assets, to include the risk of re-tasking due to other priorities.

(15) Inability to remove or penetrate command and control barriers to task across operating echelons.

(16) Inability to gain visibility into, and task, latent collector capacity.

(17) Inability to change the weight or emphasis of an existing (but uncollected) collection requirement to reflect "piggybacking" of additional collection requirements.

(18) Inability to ensure the "stale" and/or underperforming requirements are identified and removed.

3. Joint Capabilities Document for Battlespace Awareness in Joint Urban Operations

a. This document described capability needs, capability gaps, and recommendations for follow-on functional solutions analysis work pursuant to actuating battlespace awareness (BA) capabilities as described in the *Joint Urban Operations Joint Integrating Concept*.

b. The five highest priority battlespace awareness capability gaps identified are discussed below. Note: The first three of these five gaps especially pertain to persistent surveillance.

(1) **Completeness in Collection/Gathering**. Limited ability to collect and gather data and information to satisfy the unique information and intelligence requirements of an urban system, to include embedded adversaries.

(2) **Integration of Collection/Gathering**. Limited ability to integrate collection and gathering of data and information using all available assets (e.g., HUMINT, SIGINT, GEOINT, etc.) and sources (e.g., engineers, meteorologists, medical, logistics, civil affairs, other government agencies, nongovernmental organizations, international organizations, SOF, etc.) on an urban system, to include embedded adversaries.

(3) **Persistent Surveillance**. Limited ability to achieve surveillance of specific areas, at required dwell times and/or revisit rates, in order to assess the unique functions, processes, and structures (human and physical) of an urban system, and those of embedded adversaries.

(4) **Completeness of Processing, Exploitation, Analysis, and Estimates**. Limited ability to provide a complete analysis or estimate of the unique and complex functions, processes, and structures of the urban system and its embedded adversaries.

(5) **Timeliness of Processing, Exploitation, Analysis, and Estimates**. Limited ability to process, exploit, analyze and estimate at a pace required to support joint force operations and plans, and other collaborative activities, in rapidly changing urban systems.

4. **US Joint Forces Command Joint Center for Operational Analysis Studies**

a. *Operation Iraqi Freedom (OIF) – October to December 2007 Counterinsurgency Targeting and Intelligence, Surveillance, and Reconnaissance*, March 2008. This product reported that in task force operations, persistent coverage of the target was typically achieved through airborne FMV, both manned and unmanned platforms. However, brigades did not have access to the same range and depth of FMV assets, whether external or organic. Additionally, FMV usefulness was dependent, in part, upon geography. For example, in rural areas the noise from Shadow unmanned aerial vehicles (UAVs) could potentially alert the target.

b. Operation Iraqi Freedom, Joint Tactical Environment product, December 2008. Concerning ISR Operations, this product reported the following "Specific Best Practices" and solutions (i.e. "What Can Be Done?")

(1) **Best Practices**

(a) Massed FMV assets synchronized with other ISR capabilities, provided near continuous surveillance of decisive areas.

(b) Visibility of sensor data, enabled by distributed PED operations across multiple echelons, improved the development of actionable targeting and the rapid allocation of assets.

(2) **What Can Be Done?**

(a) Link in theater systems and sensors into current architectures for common situational awareness.

(b) Ensure communications gear is compatible across the services and close gaps between existing communications media (e.g. Link 16, FMV; single-channel ground and airborne radio system {SINGARS}; SIPR; mIRC).

(c) Explore the use of common-use material solutions to simplify C2 architectures.

5. **Operation Iraqi Freedom After Action Report**

Second Battalion, 24th Marines' "OIF 08-01 After Action Report," Enclosure 1. Intelligence, Surveillance, and Reconnaissance (ISR) Requests, August 2008 reported the following: Collection assets should be placed in direct support of each battalion. This would enable battalions to create collection plans based on need and not on availability of the asset. With the collection asset in direct support, the supported battalion could dictate the time of coverage based on the collection requirements. The supported battalion would also be able to dynamically re-task the assets based on changing conditions on the ground and current reporting. This would allow the supported battalion to work directly with the asset operators to ensure that the collection asset is being used in the most efficient manner. Additionally, multiple target decks should be prepared to adequately meet last minute allocations of assets.

APPENDIX F
REFERENCES

Development of this handbook is based upon the following primary references.

1. **U.S. Government Documents**

   a. Government Accountability Office (GAO). *GAO Report, GAO-07-836: Unmanned Aircraft Systems, Advance Coordination and Increased Visibility Needed to Optimize Capabilities*, July 2007.

2. **Department of Defense and Joint Chiefs of Staff Issuances**

   a. Department of Defense. *2006 Quadrennial Defense Review*, February 2006. "Intelligence, Surveillance, Reconnaissance (ISR)," pages 55-58.

   b. Department of Defense. *2010 Quadrennial Defense Review*, February 2010. "Succeed in Counterinsurgency, Stability and Counterterrorism Operations," page 22.

   c. Department of Defense. *Capstone Concept for Joint Operations*, Version 3.0, January 2009.

   d. Department of Defense. *Defense Collection Management Doctrine, Organization, Training, Materiel, Leadership and Education, Personnel, Facilities and Policy (DOTMLPF-P) Change Recommendation*, 05 May 2010 Draft on SIPRNET.

   e. Department of Defense, Joint Requirements Oversight Council (JROC). *Joint Capabilities Document for Battlespace Awareness in Joint Urban Operations*, Draft Version 0.4, 08 July 2008.

   f. Department of Defense. *Persistent Intelligence, Surveillance, and Reconnaissance: Planning and Direction Joint Integrating Concept, Version 1.0*, March 2007.

   g. Joint Chiefs of Staff. *Joint Chiefs of Staff Persistent Intelligence, Surveillance and Reconnaissance (ISR) Joint Capabilities Document (JCD)*, November 2007.

3. **Joint Publications**

   a. JP 1, *Doctrine for the Armed Forces of the United States*.

   b. JP 1-02, *DOD Dictionary of Military and Associated Terms*.

   c. JP 2-0, *Joint Intelligence*.

   d. JP 2-01, *Joint and National Intelligence Support to Military Operations*.

e. JP 2-01.3, *Joint Intelligence Preparation of the Operational Environment.*

f. JP 2-03, *Geospatial Intelligence Support to Joint Operations.*

g. JP 3-0, *Joint Operations.*

h. JP 3-05.1, *Joint Special Operations Task Force Operations.*

i. JP 3-07.4, *Joint Counterdrug Operations.*

j. JP 3-26, *Counterterrorism.*

k. JP 3-33, *Joint Task Force Headquarters.*

l. JP 3-50, *Personnel Recovery.*

m. JP 3-60, *Joint Targeting.*

n. JP 5-0, *Joint Operation Planning.*

4. Service Doctrinal Publications

a. FM 34-2 (FMI 2-01), *Intelligence, Surveillance and Reconnaissance Synchronization*, November 2008.

b. Headquarters Air Force ISR Agency. *Intelligence, Surveillance, and Reconnaissance (ISR) CONOPS Draft*, March 2008.

c. Headquarters Air Force. Air Force Doctrinal Document 2-9, *Intelligence, Surveillance, and Reconnaissance Operations.*

d. FM 3-04.15/NTTP 3-55.14/AFTTP 3-2.64, *Multi-Service Tactics, Techniques, and Procedures for Unmanned Aircraft Systems (UAS)*, August 2006.

e. Department of Army. *2010 Army Posture Statement.*

5. Combatant Command Documents

a. USJFCOM Joint Center for Operational Analysis (JCOA). *Operation Iraqi Freedom – October to December 2007 Counterinsurgency Targeting and Intelligence, Surveillance, and Reconnaissance (CTI)*, March 2008.

b. USJFCOM Joint Center for Operational Analysis (JCOA*). Operation Iraqi Freedom, Joint Tactical Environment (JTE)*, December 2008.

c.   USJFCOM J-9, *Joint Integrated Persistent Surveillance (JIPS) in Empire Challenge 2010*, version 1.0, 13 October 2010.

6. **Other**

a.   Brown, Herbert A., VADM, USN (Ret), *Sensors and Sensibility*, Signal Online, April 2006.

b.   Flynn, M.T., R. Juergens, and T.L. Cantrell, *Employing ISR: SOF Best Practices*, Joint Force Quarterly, Third Quarter 2008.

c.   Pendall, David W., MAJ, USA, *The Promise of Persistent Surveillance: What are the Implications for the Common Operating Picture?* United States Army School of Advanced Military Studies, United States Army Command and General Staff College, Fort Leavenworth, Kansas, AY 04-05.

d.   Second Battalion, 24th Marines, *Operation Iraqi Freedom (OIF) 08-01 After Action Report," Enclosure 1. Intelligence, Surveillance, and Reconnaissance (ISR) Requests.* August 2008.

Intentionally Blank

APPENDIX G
ENDNOTES

[1] JP 2-0, *Joint Intelligence*, 22 June 2007, paragraph b, page III-14.

[2] JP 2-01.3, *Joint Intelligence Preparation of the Operational Environment*, 16 June 2009, Overview, page xi.

[3] JP 3-60, *Joint Targeting*, 13 April 2007, page II-4, subparagraph c, "Target Development."

[4] JP 2-01, *Joint and National Intelligence Support to Military Operations*, 7 October 2004, page III-15 & 16, paragraph 13.

[5] The Promise of Persistent Surveillance: What are the Implications for the Common Operating Picture? A Monograph by Major David W. Pendall, United States Army School of Advanced Military Studies, United States Army Command and General Staff College, Fort Leavenworth, Kansas, AY 04-05, page 35, paragraph: Persistent Surveillance: Implications for the Common Operating Picture.

[6] Joint Publication 1-02, Department of Defense Dictionary of Military and Associated Terms, available at <http://www.dtic.mil/doctrine/dod_dictionary/>.

[7] Internal problems are defined as issues that impact PS operations which are in the JFC's control. Some examples of internal problems include maintenance problems, mission cancelations due to lack of equipment or personnel, poor mission planning, poor mission execution, too complex a mission, inaccurate geo-location, system failures, communication difficulties, etc.

[8] External problems are defined as issues that impact PS operations that are not under the JFC's control. Some examples of external problems include weather, target obscured due to haze/smoke, target is foliage/terrain masked, and other environmental factors that cannot be affected by human intervention.

[9] PS Objectives are goals that enable operational objectives. These objectives are a fusion of the PS mission, derived from the desired military end state, and the commander's guidance and intent for PS missions. PS Objectives are centrally planned and de-centrally executed to achieve operational objectives. PS Objectives provide the "what" and "why" for PS mission planners and forces engaged in PS operations, as well as offer a mechanism on how to prioritize PS operations with other military operations.

[10] The PS operation process includes the planning and directing aspects of the operation as well as the actual physical collecting of the information and the PED process.

Intentionally Blank

GLOSSARY
PART I - ABBREVIATIONS AND ACRONYMS

AO	area of operations
ATO	air tasking order
BDE	brigade
BN	battalion
C2	command and control
CAOC	combined air operations center
CCDR	combatant commander
CCIR	commander's critical information requirement
CDR	commander
CIE	collaborative information environment
COA	course of action
COG	center of gravity
COM	collection operations management
CONOPS	concept of operations
COP	common operational picture
CRM	collection requirements management
DIA	Defense Intelligence Agency
DIOCC	Defense Intelligence Operations Coordination Center
DOD	Department of Defense
DOTMLPF	doctrine, organization, training, materiel, leadership and education, personnel, and facilities
EEI	essential element of information
F2I	find, fix, and identify
FMV	full motion video
FOR	field of regard
FOV	field of view
GAO	Government Accounting Office
GCCS	Global Command and Control System
GEOINT	geospatial intelligence
HUMINT	human intelligence
HVT	high-value target
IC	intelligence community
IMINT	imagery intelligence
IRC	internet relay chat
ISR	intelligence, surveillance, and reconnaissance

J-2	intelligence directorate of a joint staff; intelligence staff section
J-3	operations directorate of a joint staff; operations staff section
JCMB	joint collection management board
JFC	joint force commander
JFCC-ISR	Joint Functional Component Command for Intelligence, Surveillance, and Reconnaissance
JIPCL	joint integrated prioritized collection list
JIPOE	joint intelligence preparation of the operational environment
JIPS	joint integrated persistent surveillance
JP	joint publication
JTF	joint task force
MASINT	measurement and signature intelligence
MOE	measure of effectiveness
MOP	measure of performance
NAI	named area of interest
OE	operational environment
OIF	Operation Iraqi Freedom
OPAREA	operational area
OPCON	operational control
OPLAN	operation plan
OSINT	open-source intelligence
PED	processing, exploitation, and dissemination
PIR	priority intelligence requirement
POC	point of contact
PS	persistent surveillance
RC	regional command
RFI	request for information
RSTA	reconnaissance, surveillance, and target acquisition
SIGINT	signals intelligence
SINGARS	single-channel ground-air radio system
SIPRNET	SECRET Internet Protocol Router Network
SOF	special operations forces
TACON	tactical control
TCPED	tasking, collection, processing, exploitation, and dissemination
TSA	target system analysis
TTP	tactics, techniques, and procedures

UAS	unmanned aircraft system
UAV	unmanned aerial vehicle
UDOP	user defined operational picture

PART II - TERMS AND DEFINITIONS

air tasking order — A method used to task and disseminate to components, subordinate units, and command and control agencies projected sorties, capabilities and/or forces to targets and specific missions. Normally provides specific instructions to include call signs, targets, controlling agencies, etc., as well as general instructions. Also called **ATO**. (JP 1-02)

assessment — 1. A continuous process that measures the overall effectiveness of employing joint force capabilities during military operations. 2. Determination of the progress toward accomplishing a task, creating an effect, or achieving an objective. 3. Analysis of the security, effectiveness, and potential of an existing or planned intelligence activity. (JP 1-02)

asset (intelligence) — Any resource--person, group, relationship, instrument, installation, or supply--at the disposition of an intelligence organization for use in an operational or support role. Often used with a qualifying term such as agent asset or propaganda asset. (JP 1-02)

center of gravity — The source of power that provides moral or physical strength, freedom of action, or will to act. Also called **COG**. (JP 1-02)

collection operations management — The authoritative direction, scheduling, and control of specific collection operations and associated processing, exploitation, and reporting resources. Also called **COM**. (JP 1-02)

collection requirement — 1. An intelligence need considered in the allocation of intelligence resources. Within the Department of Defense, these collection requirements fulfill the essential elements of information and other intelligence needs of a commander, or an agency. 2. An established intelligence need, validated against the appropriate allocation of intelligence resources (as a requirement) to fulfill the essential elements of information and other intelligence needs of an intelligence consumer. (JP 1-02)

commander's critical information requirement — An information requirement identified by the commander as being critical to facilitating timely decision-making. The two key elements are friendly force information requirements and priority intelligence requirements. Also called **CCIR**. (JP 1-02)

common operational picture — A single identical display of relevant information shared by more than one command. A common operational picture facilitates collaborative planning and assists all echelons to achieve situational awareness. Also called **COP**. (JP 1-02)

concept of operations — A verbal or graphic statement that clearly and concisely expresses what the joint force commander intends to accomplish and how it will be done using available resources. The concept is designed to give an overall picture of the operation. Also called **commander's concept** or **CONOPS**. (JP 1-02)

course of action — 1. Any sequence of activities that an individual or unit may follow. 2. A possible plan open to an individual or commander that would accomplish, or is related to the accomplishment of the mission. 3. The scheme adopted to accomplish a job or mission. 4. A line of conduct in an engagement. 5. A product of the Joint Operation Planning and Execution System concept development phase and the course-of-action determination steps of the joint operation planning process. Also called **COA**. (JP 1-02)

direct support — A mission requiring a force to support another specific force and authorizing it to answer directly to the supported force's request for assistance. Also called **DS**. (JP 1-02)

end state — The set of required conditions that defines achievement of the commander's objectives. (JP 1-02)

essential elements of information — The most critical information requirements regarding the adversary and the environment needed by the commander by a particular time to relate with other available information and intelligence in order to assist in reaching a logical decision. Also called **EEIs**. (JP 1-02)

event — An event is a national or international occurrence assessed as unusual and viewed as potentially having an adverse impact on US national interest and national security. The recognition of the event as a problem or potential problem follows from the observation. (Definition used only in this handbook, not in JP 1-02)

high-value target — A target the enemy commander requires for the successful completion of the mission. The loss of high-value targets would be expected to seriously degrade important enemy functions throughout the friendly commander's area of interest. Also called **HVT**. (JP 1-02)

intelligence — The product resulting from the collection, processing, integration, evaluation, analysis, and interpretation of available information concerning foreign nations, hostile or potentially hostile forces or elements, or areas of actual or potential operations. The term is also applied to the activity which results in the product and to the organizations engaged in such activity. (JP 1-02)

intelligence, surveillance, and reconnaissance – An activity that synchronizes and integrates the planning and operation of sensors, assets, and processing, exploitation, and dissemination systems in direct support of current and future operations. This is an integrated intelligence and operations function. Also called **ISR**. (JP 1-02)

intelligence, surveillance, and reconnaissance visualization — The capability to graphically display the current and future locations of intelligence, surveillance, and reconnaissance sensors, their projected platform tracks, vulnerability to threat capabilities and meteorological and oceanographic phenomena, fields of regard, tasked collection targets, and products to provide a basis for dynamic re-tasking and time-sensitive decision making. Also called **ISR visualization**. (JP 1-02)

ISR Enterprise — Those defense organizations, resources, and personnel assigned responsibilities for executing any part of the intelligence mission. The ISR Enterprise includes a core set of organizations and resources that have intelligence as their primary function. The ISR Enterprise may include other resources providing information of intelligence value under command and control arrangements specified by the CCDR, JFC, or subordinate/component commander. (Persistent ISR Planning and Direction Joint Integrating Concept Version 0.9) (Definition used only in this handbook, not in JP 1-02)

ISR task — A specific mission given to an intelligence discipline or collector that will support the accomplishment of desired effects and objectives. (Definition used only in this handbook, not in JP 1-02)

joint intelligence preparation of the operational environment — The analytical process used by joint intelligence organizations to produce intelligence estimates and other intelligence products in support of the joint force commander's decision-making process. It is a continuous process that includes defining the operational environment; describing the impact of the operational environment; evaluating the adversary; and determining adversary courses of action. Also called **JIPOE**. (JP 1-02)

joint operation planning process — An orderly, analytical process that consists of a logical set of steps to analyze a mission; develop, analyze, and compare alternative courses of action against criteria of success and each other; select the best course of action; and produce a joint operation plan or order. Also called **JOPP**. (JP 1-02)

measure of effectiveness — A criterion used to assess changes in system behavior, capability, or operational environment that is tied to measuring the attainment of an end state, achievement of an objective, or creation of an effect. Also called **MOE**. (JP 1-02)

measure of performance — A criterion used to assess friendly actions that is tied to measure task accomplishment. Also called **MOP**. (JP 1-02)

named area of interest — The geospatial area or systems node or link against which information that will satisfy a specific information requirement can be collected. Named areas of interest are usually selected to capture indications of adversary courses of action, but also may be related to conditions of the operational environment. Also called **NAI**. (JP 1-02)

objective — 1. The clearly defined, decisive, and attainable goal toward which every operation is directed. 2. The specific target of the action taken (for example, a definite terrain feature, the seizure or holding of which is essential to the commander's plan, or, an enemy force or capability without regard to terrain features). (JP 1-02)

operational control — Command authority that may be exercised by commanders at any echelon at or below the level of combatant command. Operational control is inherent in combatant command (command authority) and may be delegated within the command. Operational control is the authority to perform those functions of command over subordinate forces involving organizing and employing commands and forces, assigning tasks, designating objectives, and giving authoritative direction necessary to accomplish the mission. Operational control includes authoritative direction over all aspects of military operations and joint training necessary to accomplish missions assigned to the command. Operational control should be exercised through the commanders of subordinate organizations. Normally this authority is exercised through subordinate joint force commanders and Service and/or functional component commanders. Operational control normally provides full authority to organize commands and forces and to employ those forces as the commander in operational control considers necessary to accomplish assigned missions; it does not, in and of itself, include authoritative direction for logistics or matters of administration, discipline, internal organization, or unit training. Also called **OPCON**. (JP 1-02)

operational environment — A composite of the conditions, circumstances, and influences that affect the employment of capabilities and bear on the decisions of the commander. Also called **OE**. (JP 1-02)

priority intelligence requirement — An intelligence requirement, stated as a priority for intelligence support, that the commander and staff need to understand the adversary or the operational environment. Also called **PIR**. (JP 1-02)

surveillance — The systematic observation of aerospace, surface, or subsurface areas, places, persons, or things, by visual, aural, electronic, photographic, or other means. (JP 1-02)

synchronization — 1. The arrangement of military actions in time, space, and purpose to produce maximum relative combat power at a decisive place and time. 2. In the intelligence context, application of intelligence sources and methods in concert with the operation plan to ensure intelligence requirements are answered in time to influence the decisions they support. (JP 1-02)

tactical control — Command authority over assigned or attached forces or commands, or military capability or forces made available for tasking, that is limited to the detailed direction and control of movements or maneuvers within the operational area necessary to accomplish missions or tasks assigned. Tactical control is inherent in operational control. Tactical control may be delegated to, and exercised at any level at or below the level of combatant command. Tactical control provides sufficient authority for controlling and directing the application of force or tactical use of combat support assets within the assigned mission or task. Also called **TACON**. (JP 1-02)

unity of effort — Coordination and cooperation toward common objectives, even if the participants are not necessarily part of the same command or organization – the product of successful unified action. (JP 1-02) (Note: The discussion and definition of "unity of effort" in JP 2-0 is quite different, but this is the official doctrinal definition in JP 1-02, which is sourced to JP 1-0.)

Intentionally Blank